HEALING A FRACTURED WORLD

HEALING A FRACTURED WORLD

Revolutionary Poets Brigade

Edited by
Kristina Brown
John Curl
Karen Melander-Magoon
Barbara Paschke

Kallatumba Press
San Francisco, CA

http://revolutionarypoetsbrigade.org/
Printed in the United States of America.

CONTENTS

VISUAL ARTISTS

Front Cover: ANDRENA ZAWINSKY
Back Cover: LUIS GARCIA, *"The Four Seasons"*
Cover Design: KRISTINA BROWN
p. 36: BARBARA BYERS
p. 49: NAHID ARIA, *"Hands"*
p. 71: VIRGINIA BARRETT, *"FoxesNotFirearms"*
p. 63: CAROL DENNEY, *"Pregnant and in Jail"*
p. 76: ANDRENA ZAWINSKY
p. 82: ADRIAN ARIAS, *"where my dead people go"*
p. 93: AGNETA FALK
p. 122: OSCAR LOCATELLI
p. 147: KARL WIENER
p. 160: BARBARA BYERS
p. 167: SANDRO SARDELLA

PRODUCTION

Proofreading: BARBARA PASCHKE
Layout: JOHN CURL

HEALING A FRACTURED WORLD

PREFATORY

Because poetry can transcend all divisions, the Revolutionary Poets Brigade invited poets from all over the planet, speakers of many languages, to explore what can be done to heal our vulnerable world.

Over countless eons, life on earth has evolved through fire and deluge, from microscopic life to us humans, with soaring aspirations and tragic follies.

Our advancing technology has always held the promise of prosperity for all, and goods are produced in what would have been unimaginable quantities for most of human history. But we do not make the decisions about their production or consumption fairly and wisely. We seldom ask what the real cost to the planet and the human community is. While many starve, the biosphere is disrupted, and the world is stripped of its resources.

We humans, who once painted images on the walls of caves and relied mainly on the spoken word to communicate, moved on through modern printing and digital libraries and now have vast stores of knowledge at our fingertips. Messages can flash around the planet and reach others in a moment.

But many people exist more and more in an echo chamber and hear only the messages that validate their preconceptions.

Poetry opens eyes and minds. Poetry can help us heal and see the world and its challenges through different lenses.

In the following pages you will find threads of truth and inspiration that will help our planet thrive and human society come to its senses.

Jack Hirschman presente!

Editors
Kristina Brown, John Curl,
Karen Melander-Magoon, Barbara Paschke

HEALING A FRACTURED WORLD

.

TONY ALDORANDO

700 PEOPLE

This morning
While staring
Into my cup of coffee

I saw 700 people
With picket signs...

People shouting from a truck
Painful signs in rhyme...

People always feeling stuck...

It's a sign of the times

At work, you gotta beg the boss
For an extra buck

It's a sign of the times

Always
Shit, outta luck...

It's a sign of the times

No wonder I see
700 people
With picket signs...

Now it's inflation...

It's a sign of the times

Now I'm walking around the house
Looking for nickels and dimes

And now
they wanna make
A homeless encampment
A crime?

Now it's 700 people
plus one!

Out on the street
With a picket sign.

ADRIÁN ARIAS (*Peru/USA*)

POEMA DE AMOR SECRETO
*Dedicado a todos mis amigos que necesitan un
poema de amor en este momento-*

He comenzado este poema tantas veces.
cierro los ojos y solo te veo a ti

la luz de tu piel
es la comida de mi dia

tu caminar es música
y me haces respirar vida

es por eso que
permanecer en silencio frente a ti
es mi poema

Perdóname
por no poder decirte
pero tu eres todo para mi.

ADRIÁN ARIAS   *(Peru/USA)*

SECRET LOVE POEM
*Dedicated to all my friends who need
a love poem right now-*

I have started this poem so many times
I close my eyes and I only see you

the light of your skin
is the food of my day

you walking is music
and you make me breathe life

that is why
staying silent in front of you
is my poem.

Forgive me
for not being able to tell you
but you are everything for me.

AYO AYOOLA-AMALE *(Nigeria)*

THE GREAT DYING

Once upon many yesterdays, we thought,
Over many unforgotten vanished days
We thought —
they cannot change, as night changes to day,
No change in change that do muddle minds
Yet, they have changed.
They change like the many changes that occur to the fetus
They think water smells bad, so an order was given to get
                                                      water killed
They love us like we love our Christmas Turkey caringly
And yet we cannot tell what they want from us.
The flora and fauna roots are soaked with fossils;
the lungs of fishes and rivers clog with freezing plastic.
Far more than ten billion ears hear
War playing his lyre, wooing many with his song
These vipers, and make war babies they put out of the
                                                      light,
What we see are but caricatures born to our desire
Not thinking of the present or future ending
they made for themselves a plow-land buried landmines
They have drunk the only oasis
in the parched village which we were preparing
to resuscitate, to find our head
and run from a world of crack
To live far from wild criminality.
That stinks like a stagnant sea
This morning, tall, tall shabby trees shed
layers of crumpled leaves in preparation for spring.
with head nestled in good, the world grew honest,

While on their horses in iron armors the moonlight shone
                                   on their icy hearts
breathing lights cut through numbing minds
to stop another great dying.
... there went up a muffled roar
And we danced while watching a new dawn unfold
from the cruel violent storm waves, hearts are light.

MAHNAZ BADIHIAN   *(Iran/USA)*

I'LL BE AGAIN.

I'm a reborn woman.
I'll never leave my roots.
Silence doesn't turn me off.

I'll spark,
 from the depths of the ashes.
I'll draw flames,
 from the end of the blackout.

I've never died of stoning,
from rape.

Of the violence
in the dungeons of history.
From the living graves.

I'm back.
 I bloomed again.
Towards the light

LISBIT BAILEY

IT'S THE BIG LOVE IT

ONE IT, TRUE IT, THIS IS IT
IT'S THE BIG LOVE IT
IT'S FOR EACH & EVERY ONE IT IT

EARTH'S MADE OF IT, SUN STARS SPACE IT
GALAXY UNIVERSE IT
IT'S EXTRAORDINARY IT

NO IT U LOVER!
I'M MADE OF IT
YOU'RE MADE OF IT IT

I'M WRITING WITH IT, FULL OF WORDS ISN'T IT?
NOUN & VERB IT, SUBJECT & OBJECT IT
& ALL THE COLORS IT IT

DO THE CHORES IT, MAKE DINNER IT
RIDE THE BUS IT, WALK THE DOG IT
PET THE CAT IT,
BE KIND TO OTHERS IT IT

ITS NOT JUST FOR YOU & ME IT
SO PLANT IT FISH IT HOUND IT PARROT IT
APE IT GRIN & BEAR IT YOU WON'T OUTFOX IT
DON'T SQUIRREL IT AWAY IT
SHARE IT! IT

BRING THE KIDS MOM DAD OLD WEIRD GEORGIE ALONG IT
COME OUT & PLAY IT HOT POTATO IT
TAG YOU'RE IT IT

BECAUSE BIG LOVE IS IT, ISN'T IT?
IT NEVER WASN'T IT IT

WHERE WOULD I BE WITHOUT IT? COME ON & SHOUT IT
GO AHEAD & OUT IT IT

LIVE A LIFE WITHOUT IT & LOOK WHERE THAT GETS YOU IT
TOO MANY LOSING OUT ON IT FROM THEIR VERY BEGINNINGS
                                                                IT
OR ANYWHERE ALONG THE WAY IT IT

IT WAS ALWAYS THE BIG IT! NEVER LITTLE, SMALL OR TINY IT
IT's THE BIGGEST THING EVER IT! ITS WHAT MAKES LIFE
                                            MEANINGFUL IT IT

THEY KEEP TRYING TO SELL IT TO US IT BUT
YOU CAN'T BUY THE REAL THING IT! YOU CAN'T EAT IT OR
                                                        DRINK IT
OR FILL THAT HOLE INSIDE YOU IT OR SLIP IT ON YOUR FOOT IT
IT WON'T WEAR OUT IT IT'S PRICELESS ISN'T IT? IT

IT MAY WAX & WANE LIKE THE MOON IT
BUT IT NEVER DISAPPEARS IT IT

ITS JUST THERE IN THE HEART OF EVERYTHING IT
& EVERY LIVING THING'S GOT A HEART IT IT
SO SAVE SOME FOR YOURSELF IT
THEN WRAP THE REST & GIVE IT AWAY IT IT

EVERYONE DIES BUT NOT IT, FOREVER IT WILL LAST IT
BELIEVE IN IT THEN YOU'LL SEE IT IN EVERY ONE IT
EVERY CHANCE YOU GET IT COS ITS THE BIG LOVE IT
ISN'T IT? IT IT IT

KEMLYN TAN BAPPE   *(Singapore/USA)*

WHEN I WAS EIGHT

I dreamt the same dream for several nights. I saw the children of the world weeping. I woke up each night drenched in tears:

 "Why are they crying?" I begged.

"Because they don't know they are loved."

I made a child's promise that I would tell each of them. I tried time and again to make good that vow, but felt I always came short. I forgot to tell the little girl in the mirror she was loved, too. I am making it right.

You're enough
You are beautiful
I love you

LYNNE BARNES

TO THE NEARLY SIXTY PERCENT OF OUR TEENAGE GIRLS FEELING SAD OR HOPELESS

I wish your education came,
not inside cult-tivating herds,
but in intimate learning circles
that could banish bullying,
light lamps of empathy for you.

Inside your large sadness pod,
dear American teen girls,
look around—
almost twenty-five percent of you
have made a concrete plan
for how to kill yourselves.

Take this knowledge, risk
a reaching out to someone.
Visualize this invisible bond of
sisterhood, this strength, this
power waiting to be switched on.

Look beyond the bars
of your blue prison
toward caring strangers
fumbling at the gates for keys,
petitioning for your release.

Something's wrong with
a society that discovers
these statistics about its young.

Wrong, as in our country's
icy winds of condemnation
that leave half of all queer teens
shivering, seriously imagining
death as warm relief.

What if it's not you?
What if it's us?
Dear teen girls,
don't succumb.

See the cultural G-forces
crushing your hope. Reach
through your loneliness,
raise a finger, tap a shoulder,
touch a sleeve, grasp a hand,
let someone know.
Embrace your dazzling
I am.

VIRGINIA BARRETT

BETWEEN THE FEATHERS
OF THEIR DARK WINGS

On the roof across the street five crows
meet. They strut against the foggy sky

cawing and discussing the current state
of affairs. They wonder why humans

suffer so much, hurt so much, destroy
so much. Aware the remedy lies in the love

nestled between the feathers of their dark
wings, they remain a cranky bunch—not

always willing to share. Meanwhile,
the lemon tree in the yard I can see offers

up its yellow fruit, cars stream by on
Guerrero, and this old pole outside my

window continues to lean as if being pulled
in an endless tug-of-war by the electric

lines it holds . . . when suddenly the crows
swoop off one by one, releasing healing.

BENGT BERG   *(Sweden)*

UNTITLED I

wrapped by the night, with darkness between my toes and
                                        forgetfulness in my lap
there is so much that has come loose, lost its hold, broken
                                        down
and even more that binds and connects and imprisons
so much unused freedom,
a freedom of choice that consists of not choosing, of
                                        daring

and the kitchen table set with invisible dreams

we live our lives, we live in our names
too far away from both ourselves and each other

I carry a poet from Guatemala with me in the shape of
                                        some of his words:
we have to see with the eyes of those who are not yet
                                        born
and the rain falls, we fall, everything: forgetfulness,
                                        sorrows, dreams

I would like less freedom of choice and more necessity
less hesitation and greater courage, which belongs to
                                        those
who do not do it for their own sake,
for no other benefit than the sole one.

JUDITH AYN BERNHARD

THE POET SENDS A MESSAGE IN A BOTTLE

The bottle itself is a message

Its chipped and crazed
glass
a familiar shape

Coca-Cola made sweet
with brown sugar
from Mexico

A fad of the leisure class

The paper in the bottle is
from a mill in Kentucky

Last stop on the road
to ruin for fledgling
meth heads

Scourge of the rural poor

The pencil used to write
the message is from China

Mysterious home of
inscrutable workers

Suppliers of goods to the world

"If you receive this message,"
the poet writes

"be kind to another human on
this frail and ailing planet

And don't forget to send the
bottle out again."

DANIEL BROOKS

THE PATH THAT LIES BEFORE US

What does it mean
To be united?
The highest form of trust
& connectedness
Moving the planet forward
Leaving the darkest
Of ages behind.
What does it mean
To struggle?
The ultimate sacrifice
Giving up comfort & luxury
So that all needs are met.
One with the people.
One with all living things.
What does it mean
To be liberated?
The highest stage of freedom
Choosing life over exchange.

KRISTINA BROWN

FROM THE FIRE/PHOSPHORESCENT/4 PARTS
for all the poets who sometimes perform outdoors

1.
Phosphorescent.

I love the word
      The way it sounds
                What it means,
Giving light after the presence and then absence of
incident radiation.

But it often overwhelms every word around it.

2.
This is
A message
from the incandescent
            Liminal zone
                Where life fights death,
Where
      We give people
            Including ourselves
                Reasons to live,

The place of
      extremity
        Intensity
          where pastel glows electric

through the black.
Makes ever expanding mandalas.

3
From the fire

        Embers
            Pop
                Explode
                    Disappear.

From the fire
        Sparks
            Fly up

Mix
    With the silver stars
            above the dark blue horizon.

I blink
    See orange silhouettes

Phosphorescent

        Flowers
          Faces
            Bodies
              Spirits
of the innumerable
        adored
          dead,

The ones I loved
        while they lived.

They lift me
      Into the bright

          Darkness

4
Now
    Tonight
        Beneath the tower

brighter images of those who create,

Sing and laugh,
        yip like coyotes and proclaim,

They,
    You,
        Make complex patterns of delight,

Shine.

    Over
        The old glow.

JIM BYRON

THE POWER OF LOVE

It's Guernica come to life
  in the urban battle theater.
Lady Peace cries in the night. Will the nations' leaders
        hear her?
A dove lands on her shoulder
  and she takes it in her hand,
 Standing high on on a boulder that looks far over the
        land.

The least will be greatest and the greatest will be least.
When the power of love overcomes the love of power, the
        world will know peace.

Like birdsong in a battlefield,
    like flowers on a gravestone.
There is hope in Nature's prayer,
    despite the fire and brimstone.

The least will be greatest and the greatest will be least.
When the power of love overcomes the love of power, the
        world will know peace.

A rose petal falls in a pool of blood. A dandelion grows in
        the mud.

The least will be greatest and the greatest will be least.
When the power of love overcomes the love of power, the
        world will know peace.

GIANCARLO CAMPAGNA

OUR ACTIONS MAKE THE WORLD

even on the eve of springtime
see the swirls and undulations
of the clouds as gunpowder
or worse, cluster bombing
fractures of landscape,
towns and cities shorn
of people and buildings

inside when you press the remote
as you do the laundry
heads proclaiming
when the roads are clear
the assaults can begin again

a recurring festival of death
in the time of renewal and growth
mechanisms deep in the grain
to secure resources and disperse fear
spoken in the old languages
of violence

difficult to resolve
the combined rituals of fertility at springtime
the landscapes exploding with bloom
coupled with that of gross theft
and bloodshed

to reconcile plant growth
and the rape of the noncombatant
women, the murdering of our
little ones

tactics of war
the call for more tanks
rallying of citizenry
who are mostly afraid
of their own governance

you don't find empathy in the curriculum
nor taped to the inside lid of the emotional toolbox

where do we begin to access
those natural tendencies
of the human
we have always drawn from
to ease our suffering?

where do we locate
the ones that provide clarity
to the eye,
mercy to the hand?

we gaggle over the confusing whispers of

>*who knows what suffering might do to you*
>*if you knew it to be closer than you can feel*

knowing our actions
make the world
knowing our actions
make the world

Barbara Byers

JANET CANNON

MEMO TO AN ANGEL

dear angel of death to decency
we are not ready to invite you
to define our destiny it's just that
the deplorables have swallowed

bobblehead anti-science pills
and sipped the kool-aid of rage
serum to support lies that
choke us like chicken bones in

the throat of harmony is dying
in the arms of deception is stoking
violence even at school board
meetings their duplicity is throttling

voter access as they defy safe
store mask mandates with eff-you
insolence they're refusing vaccines
to show contempt for the rest of us

—here where fake is real
—here where truth is losing
—here where hope struggles

ATFEH CHAHARMAHALIAN   *(Iran)*

چشم هاییکه
چشم‌هایی که نمی‌درند
به چه دردم می‌خورند؟
زیبایی زوزه میانِ کوهِ گرسنه را نچشم؟
اندوهی را که توی رنگ‌های هوا تنهاست
و سرخی ناپدید در غبار
با آن خاکسترهای تشنه‌اش؟
لبالبِ تپه بعدِ ظهر می‌شود
کماکان به ناله‌های مجازی پهلوی توام
کماکان و با چای‌های نیمه‌شب آرام‌ترم
با خمیازه‌ای که دندان‌هایش برق می‌زند
و مشتی خاک
زیر بالشِ هر صبحش خاطره‌ای مخفی‌ست
مگر من چریده نشدم؟
برهوتِ گوشه‌ی اتاق ریخته‌اند که بیا!
زیر چانه‌ام نفسی مانده که بخواب!
چهار ساعت دیگر هم بخواب
پنهانِ خودت را بگو:
                  — سرد.
پنهانی به خودت بگو:
عاشقت هستم.
         — هرگز مگسی قدیمی در غبارِ گله‌ی دد نبوده‌ام.
بگو به خودت
                  — من.
دوباره نسیم
ضمیری نیاسوده را به کوه‌ها می‌زند
خبرم که بیاید
پشت پلک‌های بسته‌ام گریخته‌ام
خبرم
بسترِ گرگ را می‌گشاید
تنفسم
به طبیعت می‌گیرد
جهنمم
می‌زند
تا دوباره به هر لبخند
هزار جانور شوم.

38

ATFEH CHAHARMAHALIAN   (Iran)

EYES

Eyes that don't open wide
What use are they to me
If I don't feel the howling between hungry mountains?
The sadness that exists in the solitude of the colors of the air.
And the redness disappearing in the dust.
With its thirsty ashes
At the edge of the hill, it becomes afternoon
Still, with a virtual cry, I am next to you
Still calmer at midnight, having tea
With a yawn of shining teeth
And a bunch of dirt.
Under the pillow, every morning, a secret memory.
Didn't I graze?
They have been dropped naked into the corner of the room!
There's only a breath left under my chin to sleep!
Sleep for four hours.
Tell me your cold secret place
Tell yourself secretly:
I love you.
   – I have never been an old fly in the dust of the wild herd.
Tell yourself.
To breathe again, and
Hits unrested conscience to the mountain
When my news came.
I fled behind my closed eyelids.
My news opens the wolf's bed
My breath takes on nature
My hell beats, and
become thousands of animals with every smile

(Translated from Farsi by Mahnaz Badihian and Agneta Falk)

MARCO CINQUE   *(Italy)*

SUI SEGRETI IMPERSCRUTABILI

Sui segreti imperscrutabili
abbiamo scritto soluzioni eterne
chiamandole fede, scienza, verità
quando non sappiamo ancora
cosa provano una foglia e un fiore
o quello che di loro dice il vento

§§§

Ogni giorno una guerra
con una faccia diversa
che non sembra più guerra
ma uccide in nome della vita
e diventa la nostra stessa vita

§§§

Se assaggi il mare
riconosci il sapore delle
lacrime di chi l'ha attraversato
allora non puoi più respingere
nessuna vita che lui ti porta
perché ne morirebbe il cielo

MARCO CINQUE   *(Italy)*

WE'VE WRITTEN ETERNAL SOLUTIONS

We've written eternal solutions
on inscrutable secrets
calling them faith, science, truth
when we're still unaware of
what a leaf and a flower feel
or what the wind says about them

§§§

Every day there's a war
with a different face
that no longer looks like war
but kills in the name of life
and turns into our very life

§§§

If you taste the sea
you recognize the taste of the
tears of those who have crossed it
then you can no longer reject
any life it brings you
for it would slay the sky

(translated from Italian by Alessandra Bava)

FRANCIS COMBES   *(France)*

ELOGE ET CONDAMNATION DES MURS

Vive les murs qui soutiennent les toits
À bas les murs érigés en barrières
Vive les murs qui protègent du froid
À bas les murs qui servent de frontières
Vive les murs abritant des écoles
Et ceux des cours où courent des farandoles
À bas les murs couverts de barbelés
Faits pour barrer la voie aux réfugiés.
À bas les murs garnis de miradors
Vive les murs des chambres où l'on dort
À bas les murs qui font grandir la haine
Vive les ponts et les routes humaines
À bas les murs qui ouvrent des blessures
(Jamais les murs n'ont fait le monde sûr)
Vive les murs qu'éclairent des fenêtres
Vive les murs que le soleil pénètre
Les murs murant le monde murmurant
font de ce monde un champ de mines indigne
À bas les murs qui divisent les gens
Vive les murs où peut pousser la vigne.

FRANCIS COMBES *(France)*

PRAISE AND CONDEMNATION OF WALLS

Long live the walls that support the roofs
Down with walls erected as barriers
Long live the walls that protect against the cold
Down with walls that serve as borders
Long live the walls housing the schools
And those of classes where farandoles are danced
Down with walls covered with barbed wire
Made to block the route of the refugees
Down with walls embellished with watchtowers
Long live the walls of bedrooms
Down with walls that make hate grow
Long live the bridges and paths human take
Down with walls that open wounds
(Walls have never made the world safe)
Long live the walls lit up by windows
Long live the walls the sun penetrates
Walls walling up the whispering world
make of this world a shameful minefield
Down with walls that divide people
Long live the walls where the grapevine can climb

(translated from French by Barbara Paschke)

KITTY COSTELLO

HEALING A FRACTURED WORLD: TWO ACROSTICS

One

H   ealing our own ancestors from
E   ons past until now, holding tenderly,
A   vowing colonizers and colonized alike
L   aced together
I   n the fabric of our cells,
N   ow. Alive. Here. We
G   iven a chance to untangle countless

A   ncient karma snarls.

F   ree the prisoners within!
R   eform the imperialists!
A   ctualize true reparations in the
C   onfines of our own skins
T   il we know how to
U   ndo the harms we thoughtlessly
R   eenact on others. Reclaim
E   very madman, reprobate and thief,
D   espite seeming otherness.

W   e are flying along on this earthly
O   rb that needs our love for
R   eal, and all fellow passengers
L   onging for the very same thing.
D   are to be the one who reaches out first.

Two

H	ere's how it begins—
E	very small hand pushing all
A	t once, all in the same direction,
L	ike what it took to erect standing stones or
I	nvade all the places humans
N	ever should have set foot,
G	etting everyone on the same page

A	ll together, for the good. Can you

F	athom it? A great turning of winds
R	ighting our course,
A	ctivating all the goodness and
C	are every heart longs to offer? We are
T	iny transients among tiny transients, as
U	nlikley as anyone to be
R	eincarnated in this gnarled, ruptured,
E	xistential, earth-home
D	isaster we all face together.

W	hat better time to
O	pen wide with utmost
R	everence for every other
L	ost being seeking refuge? Please
D	rench the world with your love.

ANITA CRUZ

.......AND THE ARK FROWNED AT NOAH

one

the day I saw your city
drowned on the horizon
fear stormed my heart
as I recognized the fishes
had been men.

I know that you won't remember
the flood that washed over our
faces like a bad dream
telling Eve you fought for her
whispering into her cherry blossomy
hair, how brave you faced the
terrible carnage.

the sea came up to drown our country-
you pulled yourself above-
the Ark, one of the trusted friends
given you to float over the waves
reflecting your desire to live

as you shuffled towards me like a crab.
How can we return to where we used
to be, as memory fled from us and
our elders like a shadow. Is there a
way to heal a fractured world? We
cannot do it as the earth aligned
at the north star: icebergs cracking
and melting like sands. I dipped
my head into the water, prayed that

I will be able to surface from the
terrible drift.

I could see your face, as sunlight
poured like blood from your body:
dark, fallible flesh after the earth
drowned in 40 days and 40 nights

so deep I could smell the inside of
your mouth as the Ark tilted amd
shook with the tide, sick with fear,
sweat from your back, as drowned
creatures below called our names to
haunt us.

two

Will those floating corpses cleanse the
landscape of sin? I remember us slaves
too weary after the long days in the caves
chiseling the rocks for gold to appease
the gods. The girl you pried from her
father's arms to save her from impending
doom.

imagine us trembling inside the sturdy
Ark where animals roared and stomped
their feet and birds flapped their wings- to
shock us to thinking- as your questioning
glare will determine whom to save or to
leave behind, like the unicorn. most species
will die in the climate change, even million
after we took off from ant warriors so
obedient and loyal still. The oceans

rising and heavens will cry in 40 days and
40 nights.

terror, as you dwell on it after you saw
the heiroglyphics against the walls like
headlines of newspapers we read on.

three

We maybe past the point of no return-
the blood rolling in your groins. You
saw the hollowness in painted faces
in masquerade parties after the emptiness
of the city streets.

curling yourself on the corner, you told
me how hideous it is to ride the roller coaster.
the things you have to do in extreme weather
patterns. Will there be Spring or Summer after
the long Wintry chill?   I cannot find the skeleton
key to unlock the city's bright gate in your dream.
Even the astrologer knew the danger but kept
his mouth still.

The story how the iceberg gashed the Titanic
as if planned by the heavens. Do you remember
what we found when you were born? How our
doctor found a second heart besides your main
one, as if there is a cure if the first one died as
a new world will be there to replace it.....

Nahid Aria, *Hands*

ROMEO ALCALA CRUZ   *(Philippines/USA)*

GRETA CHIDES A SOCIETY IN DENIAL

Let me tell you: the red line is coming fast that
we may never even notice, though the icebergs are
breaking up and the oceans are rising fast.   Last
night, I dreamed a tree touched the gate of Heaven
as another firebreather of the Amazons wanted to
raze all the forests, breathing the oxygen of the
earth.   A tree stump would remain as ashes fall all
over the earth.   I wanted to heal the earth that is
fractured now beyond repair.   Almighty Father is
mad, looking at the way we spurned our world
unnecessarily.   We see what is coming but seemed
helpless anyway. Such future is no more than a
thin, ozone layer above the earth: the next
famine or hurricane as the night blankets the
flowers from the buds.

What of the children's dreams?   My friends and
contemporaries, I should ask? We dream of green,
that are now broken tables, chairs and houses
from the wars or is it the lining of the tiger's mouth?
The blood of my brothers in Ukraine or the front wall
of a fiery furnace in West Africa? Have we inclined
so far back that we cannot go forward, anymore?
Maybe it is the heart of a baboon, hyena or crocodile
in ourselves as we wanted to murder with claws,
daggers or bayonet sharp teeth? Add this to some
landscape burning black tar in Nigeria. It will be
easy to say the oracle has lost her lips after a long
deep dark sleep and then she woke up bubbling
frightening prophecies. Is there a way to heal a
world that is already broken? Just a palm reader

hiding an eye, we feigned ignorance of the signs:.
the cauldron heat in summer days and excessive
chill in winters.

No more platform of obscurity. Reject the corner of
denial in bliss! Articulate and ramble like an insane
babbling wild eyed man but only through rational action
will we be saved. The old stories with different
protagonists are here. After the last ice age, 10,000 years
ago, some relics like Gobekli of Turkey or the Sphinx of
Egypt are still here, to remind us of the past. The huge
boulders fitted together like charm.   The carved lizard on
a rock still crawls. The full chest of a bird or reptile still
expands.

Every dream comes out after the permafrost thawed out
in the Arctic to wring out memories like rags.   Why not
let them come out alive, after blanketed by mists of time.
Saber toothed tigers. Giant sloths. Mamoth bisons. And
there was Adam, first man that saw pristine nature after
heaven splits from the earth.   Even the seagull squawks
out its story after darkness tried to choke her before
dawn.

JOHN CURL

ABSORBING EVIL

"Be loving enough to absorb evil,
and understanding enough to turn
an enemy into a friend."

Understanding has always
been the basis of friendship
and understanding your enemy
has always been critical in struggle.

Sometimes enemies do become friends.
It has happened many times.
The exception that demonstrates the rule.

When I was a kid in the 1950s,
my grandpa was the only person
I knew who ever talked about revolution.
It was the McCarthy era, and radical
social change was dangerous to talk about.

Then the Civil Rights Movement exploded.

I'd already learned from my grandpa,
even before I learned again
from Martin and Malcolm and the others,
that the glue of this system is violence.

My grandpa, you see, was a communist,
from back in the 1920s and '30s.
But when building a just world
turned out to be much more elusive
than the old revolutionaries had predicted,
many of the dreamers of social justice
and solidarity forever blamed each other
and turned on each other. Then World War 2

exploded and social change
was off the table for the duration.

Beyond my grandpa,
the first people I knew who
talked about what we called
"the revolution," were other kids.
The revolution we kids talked about
—and almost believed in—
was not my grandpa's revolution of workers
seizing power and instituting social justice,
but the revolution of us seizing power
over our lives and living differently.

We're still walking along
that cultural quake fault today.
Demagogues, intent on chaos
and destruction, still stir the poisons
threatening to engulf us all,
while too many of our estranged
sisters and brothers still enable them.

Martin and Malcolm must have
understood from the beginning
that revolution is very personal
and absorbing evil
can exact a very heavy toll.

Follow that long trail of blood as it bends
along the dirt road toward justice.

*"Be loving enough to absorb evil,
and understanding enough to turn
an enemy into a friend."*

That's what MLK wrote
to the first riders of integrated busses
in Montgomery, Alabama, back in 1956.

AMIT DAHIYABADSHAH (*India*)

WHOSE REPUBLIC

One by one turn by turn
the cat and the bat and the crow and the rat
have taken my city.
Insomnia rules the night and fear of the siren and the
flasher rule the day
and that broad promised highway into the future
is taken up by the motorcades of
the politician
the shaker and mover,
the power broker,
the wheeler dealer,
the spin doctor,
the trouble shooter.

Leaving only a tiny lane for 'We the People' to navigate
our way precariously ahead.

In 75 years we the people have been broken and tamed

the have-nots have been bought with false promises

the haves have been bought with tax loopholes

the middle class is ritually slitting its own throat
upon the sharp edge of the credit card

And we the children of the Satyagrahis (the freedom
fighters)
we are doubly damned and doubly doomed
for we have not learnt to look the other way
or turn the other cheek

So shoot me thrice when my time comes

Once in the gut to balance the pain of so much
hunger and unequal living

Once in the heart for it was a fickle thing
and always too easily broken

and once in the head for always thinking the impossible
and dying to make it happen.

GARY S. DANIEL (NÈG GONBOLYEN)   *(Haiti)*

LOKSIDYÒL

Tout sa dyòl yo pa di
Se sa y ap fè je klè.
Tout sa yo fè se lekontrè
Sa w ta renmen yo fè
pou degonfle lè nitre
epi penyen pwèl domestik esklavaje,
makiyaj pou sipòte chèf plantasyon
sou labitasyon kan n pa kale
bèf pa vle kontinye an won
vire moulen
poutan men yo pije san machin alèkile;
jwèt tèt vid
tèt plen
nan makout payas ja elektwonik
san je pa wè pou detounen
kè detounen nanm
madigra mal maske tan pèdisyon
tout lè solèy pa leve
ni rasin yo ni pye bwa yo ni flè yo
p ap miltipliye anba je klan rasis
yon lè se te fòdejou
jodijou se gitmo
Dwat, gòch
Gòch, dwat
Ès, wès
bitasyon san fontyè p
lantasyon san plantè.

kè kontantman loksidyòl
sou balkon atlantis!

56

GARY S. DANIEL (NÈG GONBOLYEN)   *(Haiti)*

LOXYLIPS

All that their mouth wouldn't say
This is what they are doing clearly
Everything they do is the opposite
What you would want them to do
To deflate nitrous air
And not to combine the hair of domestic slavery,
Makeup to support plantation chiefs
On the camping grass we don't care
Cows which do not want to continue in circles
Spin milling
Yet hands are extracting without machine;
Empty brain game
Filled brain
In creating dirty electronic money straws
Absent of eyes to quilt diversion
Heart deviates soul
Madigra badly masks astray time
All the time the sun doesn't rise
Neither roots nor trees nor flowers
Will not multiply under the eyes of racist clans
Once it was at Fort de Joux
Today is Gitmo
Right, left
Left, right
East, west
Habitat without borders
Plantation without planters.

Heart happiness loxylips
On the balcony of Atlantis!

(translated from Creole by the author)

57

LUCILLE LANG DAY

THE LEGACY
For my grandchildren

I leave you the last four percent of the ancient redwoods
that once covered more than two million acres
of the California coast. Watch for Roosevelt elks,
black-tailed deer and mountain lions among the trees;
for spotted owls, marbled murrelets, flycatchers,
thrushes, jays and woodpeckers in the canopy.

I leave you the last ten thousand blue whales
of the hundreds of thousands that once roamed
the oceans, the largest animals known to have lived.
They've been recorded singing Beethoven's *Ode to Joy.*
Their huge hearts beat only twice per minute
when they dive beneath the surface of the sea.

I leave you a watery planet, now warming
because humans are so dependent on oil and coal.
Wildfires turn the sky orange and drive away birds
while flash floods shatter houses and trees in their path.
May your generation create a world that runs
on goodwill, fairness, sunshine and wind.

I leave you a country torn by hatred and lies.
Though these are age-old problems, they must
be faced and conquered again by each new generation.
Don't believe everything you hear. People lie
for many reasons: ignorance, malice, mischief, greed.
Truth always exists somewhere, and you can find it.

I leave you the redwood in my backyard, which suffers
from *Botryosphaeria* cankers, and the Anna's

hummingbirds that visit the Mexican sage out front
while I write poems inside. I leave you those too—
brief records of my journeys, joys and sorrows.
I leave you grief. I leave you love. I leave you hope.

DIEGO DELEO   *(USA/Italy)*

THE SONG OF COURAGE

If you think of yourself as dead,
you'd have the fortitude to speak
what's been on your mind for years
and even decades burning inside you
as a flame that you continue to sing,
the song of those who have been
silenced by bullets and swords.

You'd be calling on the carpet of
shame the cowardly dictators who
took the lives of those who waved
the flag of freedom and justice.

You'd have the courage not to fear
the repercussions of those who have
perished, who are still giving voice
from the grave to the next generation
to wave the flag of freedom and justice.

VIVIAN DEMUTH

THE AGE OF EXTINCTION

A few nights ago, a bear danced around my garden carrots
          and bowed to sniff the sow's scat in the soil bed.
Last summer, a deer yanked my Tibetan prayer flags
          from fire-tower scaffolding
and paraded adorned antlers past trampled skulls
          in the broken forest.
I am a human animal walking a dirt trail of illusions
          tossing vegetable scraps a mile from fire-tower
          cabin for the closest or quickest to snack.
In my first six years of fire lookout solitude wrestling
          I saw a hungry caribou outrun a wild six-pack
          of dart-gun helicopters,
heard ravens chuckle circling above loggers'
          orange flagging tape alit in forest flames,
followed a scarred moose chase a fleeing Honda generator
          along another new mountain road,
and took photos of a wolf pack stealing the seismic camp's
          grilling steaks and biting off a page
          from the First Handbook of Habitat Protection.
Over the next six years from mountain heights, I've
                              watched
          the wildlife thin and the oil drills strike back.
Is this the Age of Extinction in which only Fortune's wheels
          will roll on?
I pray that some drugged grizzly will wake up and flip the
                              switch.
Can a human ever gain the insight of a drugged bear?
In the meantime, I'll sit in the petrified bedrock
          with what looks like a young dinosaur
          and write for the unwritten record.

CAROL DENNEY

PREGNANT AND IN JAIL
written June 24, 2022, after the Supreme Court's
inspirational Dobbs decision

I can see my future through my pint of ale
we all will be together now pregnant and in jail
we tried to make it happen without childcare or bail
but we'll have solidarity pregnant and in jail

CHORUS: pregnant and in jail. pregnant and in jail
let the men do all the work, we're pregnant and in jail

a woman scorned is one thing she can get pretty mad
but force her into childbirth and it can get pretty bad
she's going to start to organize it's going to happen fast
and if you all get in the way she's going to kick your butt

CHORUS: pregnant and in jail. pregnant and in jail
let the men do all the work, we're pregnant and in jail

the court has intellectuals they must have studied hard
but somehow they left women out they did it from the
                                                    start
I'm not sure what we all did wrong it is a tired tale
we're here together singing songs pregnant and in jail

            Bridge: I don't know how we pull this out I'm not
                                        sure what we do
            it's really hard to change until the men get
                                        pregnant, too
            if it's the "potential life" that gets to make the call
            why can't all the eggs I got each get a vote this fall?

we're never getting laid again the men begin to see
that all the dating apps they use are empty as can be

the court supreme has focus but watch the tables turn
it's all about the eggs right now but wait 'til it's the sperm

CHORUS: pregnant and in jail. pregnant and in jail
let the men do all the work, we're pregnant and in jail

we'll all be singing sappy songs about the days of Roe
and how we all got rounded up and how we miss them so
but here we are in county court the men can send us mail
we hope to make some license plates we're pregnant and
in jail

CHORUS: pregnant and in jail. pregnant and in jail
let the men do all the work, we're pregnant and in jail (x2)

(Video at
https://www.youtube.com/watch?v=JYNiyoO0a9o)

GERMAIN DROOGENBROODT   *(Belgium)*

ARTIFICIAL INTELLIGENCE

Rivers overflow their banks
houses are demolished
cars swept away
by the raging waters:
man has disrupted nature.

In vain
wisdom's warning words

Would a chip, implanted in the brain,
offer more wisdom or even more blindness
and indoctrination?

CARLOS RAÚL DUFFLAR

LET THE SEED OF PEACE RISE IN OUR HEARTS

Since my youth, I have lived half a century in the climate
                                                    of war
This space of time from the Atlantic waters to the
                                                    Pacific Ocean
A caravan of blood squeezes through the universe like
                                                    a ball of fire
The Earth cries for peace
Cuba, Puerto Rico, the Philippines, Korea, Vietnam,
Santo Domingo, Cambodia, Laos, Grenada, Nicaragua,
Panamá, Iraq, Afghanistan, Syria, Venezuela, Western
                                                    Sahara and Donbass
Crossing over into a circle on the other side
For a new horizon to rise
Millions are suffering homelessness and dying in the
                                                    streets
Food insecurity is the order of the day
Billions for the war machine
A rage against the war machine
A past moment of marching in Wall Street
With the High School Students Mobilization Against
                                                    the War
Verses of peace shall lift the light of love
All over the people of the world
Climbing over to the mound
Looking into the sky
Drinking a cafecito
And listening to Richie Havens sing the Peace Train
That we are in the age of darkness
And the warmongers are dancing on the edge
Of nuclear destruction of our planet
And today we are here and Spring is near

A new dawn will rise
Live in harmony together and heal
With our demand to free an old freedom fighter of SNCC
Jamil Al-Amin a/k/a Rap Brown
With paz, peace, and mir

AGNETA FALK

THE LOVE OF OTHER

In the dark times will there also be singing?
Yes, there will also be singing. About the dark times.
Bertol Brecht

Such a gift to be born
that first breath
of a perfectly innocent being
without a scrap of hate
Just waiting to be nourished,
grow and reach for the light
one little heart, one little brain
eager to learn.

What a gift to be given
what opportunity to wipe
the slate clean of hatred
and racial bile, to cut
the umbilical cord to
the murderous past
with the only weapon
worth carrying
the love of other.

MAURO FFORTISSIMO

A FRACTURE

I vote for a crack,
a large sinkhole
where to throw most senators

I vote for fracking
in congressmen and congresswomen's backyards

I vote for the ending of government
yeah, I vote for that : fire them all !

resolutions ? yup, I will run with a grenade in my pocket
through the streets of Ramallah...

how to fix this mess...?
first finish the breaking
dismantle the offices of climate deniers
fill all dumps with corporate greed
deport supremacists to Mars
with bankers and royal fucks

run run with whales and swim with giraffes
be valiant and cavaliere
wear no insignia
but the rainbow of love

I don't know what else
ban the bullet
kill the market
jail soldiers generals and colonels

to the gulag with entrepreneurs

war mongers profiteers
financial advisors wealth managers,
make Florida secede and let crocodiles have a feast,
make Texas pay, give it back to Mexico!

the ozone? the ozone...
the polar caps and bears? the polar caps and bears...
global warming? yup global warming

everything is cracking...
frontiers accords forests
there is no faking it any longer
glaciers are witness
plastic oceans
unbreathable air

how to fix it is for magicians to figure out
Titans and Gods not enough...
we need pure magic
intergalactic magic
musical magic
of the sphere
a magic so tricky no human can muster

yeah, I leave it to future generations
meaning generations with no future
to resolve the theorem,
careful reasoning needed...

March 9th, 2023
waiting for an oceanic river
to pay us a visit yet again...

MARK FISHBEIN

CODE RED FOR HUMANITY

You, who was there, tell me about the past.
Tell me about the fields of fruit trees,
The open skies filled with migrating birds
Bowing to the minions of wind.

How boundless the world must have been,
Filled with green shores and crystal peaks
Before we filled the seas with plastics
And the deepest wells with broken glass.

I live in a labyrinth of the geometric,
The air I breathe is filtered and dry.
My eyes are lazars, my blood electric,
A twenty-first century cave dweller; I live inside.

This computer takes me around the globe
To share laments for the extinctions.
The food arrives to my door from slaughterhouses
And from acres of bleached wheat and corn.

How we have voyaged on a ship of apathy
In search of new continents to plunder.
It has now been a century left to ponder
The ultimate reality of our machines.

No matter now. We cannot survive without them.
The future looms a witches shawl,
A sorcerer rant, a maniac Moses
Bringing plagues of AI.

Outside are continents of poisoned reefs,
Charred forests and frozen sands; Tell me
Of landscapes free from the touch of man,
And the world as it was outside my screen.

Virginia Barrett, *FoxesNotFirearms*

MARCOS FREITAS   *(Brazil)*

SONHOS SOMOS

uns dizem que os sonhos devem ser vividos
outros que eles devem ser divididos
já outro que sonhos sonhos são
e eu o que digo?
e eu o que sonho?

às vezes o tempo passado
me é futuro
do presente ou do pretérito
eu já nem sei?

o que esperar dos sonhos?
o que esperar do que somos?

som e sonho:
partituras atemporais.

MARCOS FREITAS   *(Brazil)*

OUR DREAMS

some say dreams should be lived;
others that they should be shared;
one might say dreams are just dreams.
and what do i say?
and what do i dream?

sometimes the past
looks like future to me …
present or past –
but who knows!

what to expect from a dream?
what to expect from who you are?

sounds and dreams –
timeless musical scores.

(Translated from Portuguese by the author)

LUIS GARCÍA *(El Salvador/USA)*

CAFÉ

En las montañas,
Las nubes suben,
Abrazan el paisaje de la jungla, brinda un respiro
vapor, calor sibilante
que rodea,
cascadas
sobre una frente sudorosa y juvenil
aspiraciones relucientes, goteo
Soñadores
Sueño
flores de Café
Frutan
LABOR
Explotado, ellos toman todo
dijo que no viniera,
sordo a la ignorancia, el se va.
Las hojas verdes
hacer eco, hablar, susurrar,
sobre los sentimientos revolucionarios
Ganando la LOTERIA
Da la OPORTUNIDAD
Negro amargo
Sin azúcar,
así lo disfrutaba mi abuela;
no es que le haya gustado el sabor amargo,
pero su vida, como su piel,
marrón oscuro del sol
ardiente, lleno de arrugas,
historia
Mi primer sorbo
Un niño
tono marrón claro,
azúcar extra,
muy dulce,
la juventud puede ser así.

LUIS GARCÍA   *(El Salvador/USA)*

COFFEE

In the mountains,
Clouds Climb,
Hug the jungle landscape, provides respite
steam, hot, hissing heat
that surrounds,
waterfalls
over a sweaty youthful brow
glistening aspirations, drip
Dreamers,
Dream
Coffee flowers
fruit
LABOR
Exploited, they take everything,
told not to come,
deaf to ignorance, he leaves.
The green leaves
echo, talk, whisper,
about Revolutionary Sentiments
Winning in LOTERIA
Gives OPPORTUNITY
Bitter Black
No Sugar,
this is how my grandmother enjoyed it;
it's not that she enjoyed the bitter taste,
but her life, like her skin,
dark brown from the Sun
ardent, full of wrinkles,
history
My first sip,
A child
light brown tone,
extra sugar,
very sweet,
youth can be this way.

Andrena Zawinsky

RAFAEL JESÚS GONZÁLEZ (*USA/Mexico*)

COMO SON LAS COSAS
AS THINGS ARE

Como son las cosas

Hemos crecidos
fuera de toda proporción,
hecho un mundo demasiado grande
para la Tierra,
fijado la mirada en los cielos
para un futuro hogar
porque hemos echado a perder
el paraíso que nos dio nacer
y ya pronto no podrá
sostener la vida.

As Things Are

We have grown
out of all proportion,
made a world too big
for the Earth,
fixed our sights to heaven
for a future home
because we have ruined
the paradise that birthed us
& soon may no longer
be able to sustain life.

ART GOODTIMES

$100 RAMBLER
from The Sixties series

One summer
Capt. Barefoot criss-crossed the country
in a faded green Rambler – the driver side door
emblazoned with a Cloud House pre-puter meme

POET TREE
is the
HEART
at
LIBERTY

Picking up every hitchhiker ready for a ride

Orin Hatch fans in Utah
Legions of the newly hippied
Runaway angels. AWOLs on the lam

The sweet old lady who sold him the wheels
made no secret of the engine's exhaust leak

Warning him to roll the windows down
rain or shine
to keep the killer monoxide at bay
which they did, the Captain & his hitchers

Bundled up in night jackets
Stripped to T-shirts by midday

Came home to Noe Valley with cooties
What is that strange bug crawling

on the chesterfield?

Parked the off-emerald artcar
for good he thought

Streetsweepers swept around Ol' Mr. Nash
Neighborhood landmark
Poetry Flash's first photo spread

Until the City changed
to weekly no park dates up & down the streets

Laid off all the union guys & bought
a pricy street-sweeping machine
that made a lot of noise

Pushed a lot of litter out & about
except for pristine clean ovals
like pavement pockmarks
of a disease nobody wanted to diagnose

All the journals from those wild years
burnt up in a Placerville pyre

Blood sacrifice the mountains demanded
if the Captain was to nest
beneath their avalanche & mudslide flanks

Dodging disasters like rockfall on Norwood Hill
Living simple on the edges of wealth

Planting trees of poetry
Sweeping leaves & grass into random
congeries of unburnt books

EGON GÜNTHER   *(Deutschland)*

IST DAS ALLES WAS WIR KÖNNEN

statt alles für alle zu geben und mehr
rennt jeder für sich dem glück hinterher

furcht brennt im herzen schweiß im genick
das menschenleben ertragen als klassengeschick

verfolgt vom schatten nahender strafen
auf ziellosen fluchten verirrt wie entflohne sklaven

ist das alles was ihr kennt
habt ihr nicht mehr zu bieten?

geschöpfe geplagt von scham und not
streitbare diener ihrer herren gebot

ein dasein als knecht in des leviathans mühle
entgangene urlaubsfreude als schlimmstes der gefühle

gierige träume vom schlaraffenland
von süßem nichtstun am weißen strand

ist das alles was wir können
haben wir nicht mehr zu bieten?

EGON GÜNTHER   *(Germany)*

IS THAT ALL WE CAN DO

instead of giving all for everyone and more
it's happiness that each one's looking for

fear burning in the heart sweating in the furrow
suffering man's lot in their social class burrow

fleeing from the shades of punishments looming
on the run like slaves in aimless flights erring

is that all you know and go for
cannot you offer more?

creatures plagued by shame and necessity
disobeying their masters' order with audacity

living as serfs in leviathan's treadmill
vacation joys missed the worst of their fill

dreaming greedily of cockaigne
of sweet loafing on white sand

is that all we can do
cannot we offer more?

(Translated from German by Jörg W. Rademacher)

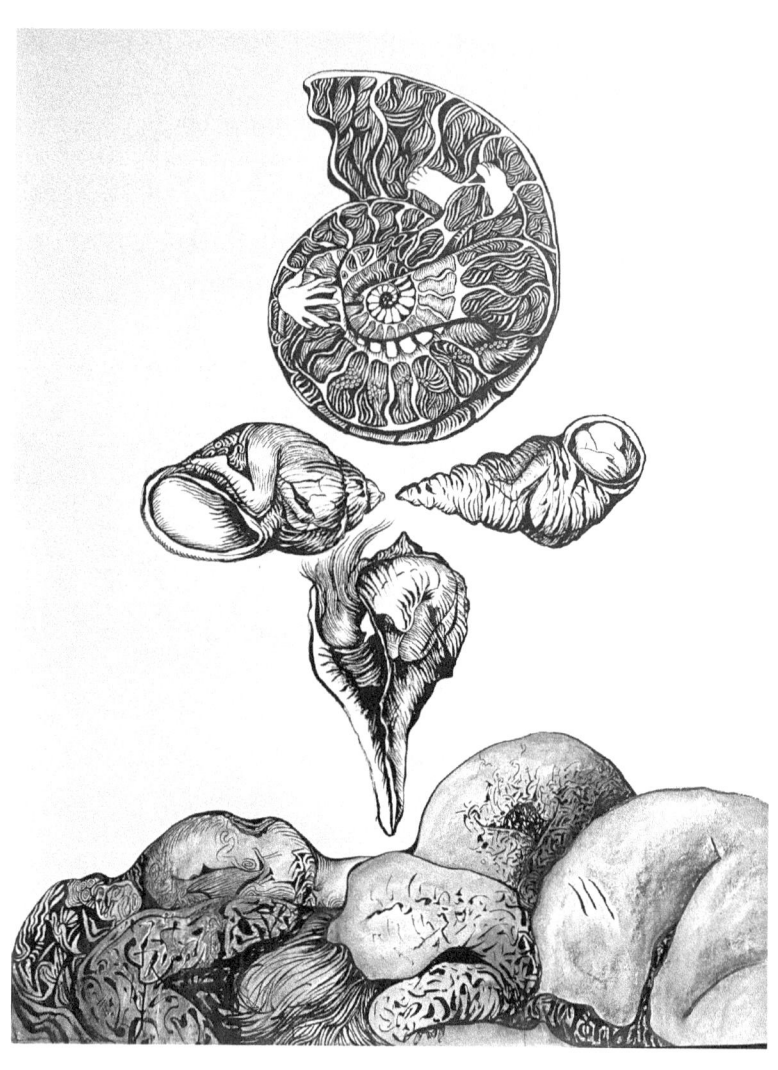

Adrian Arias, *where my dead people go*

KAMRUL HASSAN   *(Bangladesh)*

MY VILLAGE IS
A MIRROR IMAGE OF THE WORLD

I see the reflection of this world in my village
The wind of this village is not separated from
                                        the rest of the world
The water of the world is holding the hands of her water
The form of its women is exactly similar to those of others
The trees are as green and cool as the trees of the world
The clouds that float on her sky are very much like
                                        those of the world
The yellow coloured birds perching on its branches
Are the birds of another world
They are the full bodied bondage of the richness
                                        of the planet's soil.

I see the face of the world in the face of my village
The soil of this village is the print of Earth's soil and merged
The wings of her skies are touching those of the World
The current in her stream is exactly similar to
                                        those of Planet Earth
The flowers are as smiling and colourful as any other on Earth
Fishes that swim in her seas are like the seas of the world
The women who are sitting in the shrubs of this village
Are they the women of another Planet?
They are and and should be the women of the whole
                                        body of mother Earth.

I see the hibernation of the world in my village...

BILL HATCH

THE GREAT BIG BEAUTIFUL BEAST

Soles of our feet itching
Milling under the Ferry Building
Sounds of many voices
Surrounded by faces we've always known
But not by name
We who wear our hearts on our shirts
March
For another day
Hope to bring hope to the streets
Our cry, our *grito*
Breaks the fangs of
Transnational plutocracy
Sun Yat-Sen awakens and dances
In St Mary's Square
The faces of saints of all our struggles
Sail over Market Street
With the gulls and ravens
There's Jack waving from the sidewalk in his trench coat
Crystal care and love song for humanity
We hear a cocky Aussie drawl talking union
Democracy,
workers' fight for equality
to the tune of gunfire, cracked heads
bones breaking and screams,
Now his brothers march impeccably
In white caps and black friscos
Ancient Wobblies come by land
Antique Commies by sea
Ferlinghetti utters a final prayer
Warms our belly to forget our blisters
Before the street itself bellows

We Shall Overcome
Hell No We Won't Go
And El Pueblo Unido Jamás Sera Vencido

The arc of Harvey's voice surpasses
The sound of straight white bullets
His blood cries out
Along with George's blood
Dow Wilson's blood
And the blood of Counderakis and Sperry
And so many others just
Names on the blotter
Today and tomorrow and forever
We and you and we and we
Roar our love
Honor our dead
Restore
The City of our mothers
To her dignity.

We march.

"But where are Sister Mary
Boom Boom and the other
Sisters, those of Perpetual Indulgence?"
You ask
But they are here
In the coda
Dancing behind
The Emperor Norton
Strange de Jim and
A passel of streakers
In pastel sneakers.

MARTIN HICKEL

UNDER THE SUN

you who have seen too much
& forgotten even more -- still
begin each day -- a newborn
eyes squinted tight against light
bright with spectacular blossoms
oceans wrestling mountains
bowels ripped open by steel
profitable slaughter manufactures
paintings of nirvanas crafted

by hand for men so rich they
never dirty their own & villages
too poor for death to be hidden
schools of children alive with
impossible possibilities & old
used-up souls moving slowly
patiently wobbling toward stillness
explosions & healings & miracles
saints pull out of their purses or

cut & hammer together with blood
corpses & forests tangled in pieces
all sorts of amazing processes
uncovered by tireless digging
money gushing up like lava from
resources long primed to erupt
families finding joy in each other's
baskets of treats & troubles
embracing thorns tenderly

dressing every tiny wound

even a poem good for keeping
a kind of found treasure you
might uncover -- mere words
weary as they are -- strengthen
yes & things keep growing
getting bigger & going faster
than ever --- for what -- exactly
is there -- new -- under the sun

JACK HIRSCHMAN

THE HOME ARCANE
(for the National Union of the Homeless)

1.
Winter has come. In doorways, in alleys, at the top
of church steps,
under cardboard, under rag-blankets
or, if lucky, in plastic sacks,
after another day of humiliation,
sleeping, freezing,
isolated, divided, penniless,
jobless, wheezing, dirty
skin wrapped around cold bones,
that's us, that's us in the USA,
hard concrete, cold pillow,
where fire? where drink?
Damned stiffs in a drawer
soon if, and who cares?
Shudders so familiar to us,
shivers so intimate, our hands finally
closed in clench after another day
panhandling, tongues hanging out;
dogs ate more today, are curled
at the feet of beds, can belch, fart,
have hospitals they can be taken to,
they'll come out of houses and sniff
us dead one day,
pieces of shit lying scattered here
in an American city
renowned for its food and culture.

2.
The concrete is our sweat hardened,
the bridge our vampirized blood;
the downtown, Tenderloin and Broadway
lights - our corpuscles transformed into ads:
our pulse-beat the sound *tengtengenteng*
of coins piling up on counters, in
phone-booths, BART machines, *tengtengenteng*
in parking meters, pinball contraptions,
public lavatories, toll booths;
our skin converted into dollar bills,
plastic cards, banknotes, lampshades
for executive offices, newspapers, toilet-paper;
our heart—the bloody organ the State
gobbles like a geek in a sideshow
that's become a national circus of the damned.

O murderous system of munitions and inhuman rights I
That has plundered our pockets and dignity;
O enterprise of crime that calls us criminals,
terrrorism that cries we are fearful,
greed that evicts us from places we ourselves have built
miserable war-mongering that sentences us to misery
and public exposure as public nuisances to
keep a filthy republic clean—
This time we shall not be disappeared
In innercity ghetto barrio or morgue
This time our numbers are growing into battalions
Of united cries:

3.
We want the empty offices collecting dust!
We want the movie houses from midnite til dawn!
We want the churches opened 24 gods a day! We built
them.

They're ours. We want them!
No more doorways, garbage-pail alleys,
no more automobile graveyards,
underground sewer slums.
We want public housing!
No more rat-pit tubing, burnt-out rubble-caves,
no more rain-soaked dirt in the mouth,
empty dumpster nightmares of avalanches of trash
and broken bricks,
screams of women hallucinating at Muni entrance gates,
no more kids with death-rattling teeth under discarded
                                                          tarp.

We want public housing!
We the veterans of your insane wars,
workers battered into jobless oblivion,
the factory young: fingers crushed into handout
on Chumpchange St.,
the factory old: spat-out phlegm from the sick
corporate chest of profits.
Instead of raped respect, jobs
with enough to live on!
Instead of exile and eviction in this,
our home, our land,
Homeland once and for all
for one and all
and not just this one-legged cry
on a crutch on a rainy sidewalk.

BRUCE ISAACSON

IN A MOMENT, SOMEHOW...

At seventeen, one day, after years
watching Kung Fu on television
as if no real study was needed
just the dream to become
"a man, as other men..."
in suburban Moraga, California
I lay on the slope of a hill
in natural grass I can still feel on my ears
a rock touching the top right of my hair
I hear a plane far off it becomes
a distant music
I am lulled...
so relaxed I am near sleep
also vibrantly awake
the world stops, in a moment somehow
some bottom drops out of time
and I feel how we're all
connected— me, soft grass, rock at my head,
natural scent of the hills, disaster
and suffering in Persia, plane
in the distance, Moraga, in a moment
my heart fills with something that
never empties.
From then, many mistakes still, seeking
such a state never found
with drugs, sex, knowledge,
I live on fifty years with this memory—
never finding, or forgetting, knowing
we are all of
one body, one heart, one mind.

SUSU JEFFREY

RELATIVES

What is it about suicide
and the race?
Trees live and die
and rot in place
to nourish the next
generation.

Trees thrive in community
share nutrients
by root teats. Very
subtle. No tax write-offs
even between pines and hardwoods
no prejudice.
Consider: me in sunshine
you in shade
but if I don't feed you
we both blow down
and if I rake
then I have to fertilize,
the make-work economy.

Mo-ther trees
come on and mu-ther trees
exporters of oxygen
slurpers of rain bombs
singers in wind.

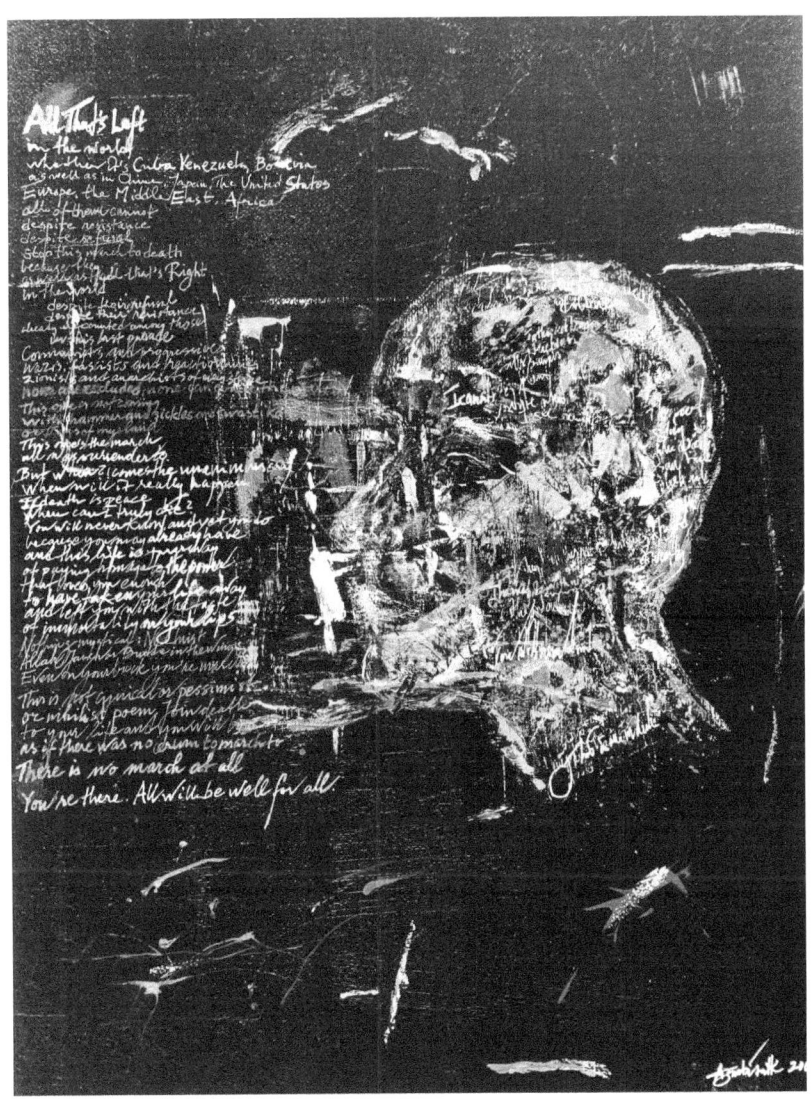

Agneta Falk

ZIBA KARBASSI   *(Iran)*

شعر از زیبا کرباسی
نامه های خصوصی ی بهادر درانی و آهو حسانی
346

مرا از بفهمت بفهم آهو
از فهمانی ات
فطرتت
از قاب عقل نه
از آفرین خانه اش
از کتابخانه نه
کنه کلمه گاه
مرا از اختصامتت بختاص
از اختصانی ات
جنمت
ائتمانت
ائتمانی ات
درونگه بی تشویش
اگر اینان همه آدمند
تو آدم نباش
چنان عشق بورز
که بزرگترین انتقامت از خیانت کار
گسستن ات باشد

ZIBA KARBASSI *(Iran)*

Letter 346
Few Words of Earth to Humanity

Know me from your knowing
Your knowledge

Understand me from your understanding
Your understood
Your nature

Not from the frame of intellect
But from the subconscious of your subconscious

Not from your library
But from the bare bones of its ink

That personal
That distinctive
That exclusive

Your genuine
Your genius

Spherical volume of trust
Unshaking outside
Uncorrupted inside

If this is humanity
Don't be human

Love in a way
That your greatest response to treachery
Is to be detached

(Translated from Farsi by Nazlee Radboy)

ELIOT KATZ

LIBERATION RECALLED #25

In the midst of early American modernism,
      35,000 workers were killed
      & over 700,000 injured
      in 1914's industrial accidents.
That year, more than 100 socialists
      elected local office
      by pure products
      of Oklahoma.
The *Brooklyn Eagle* fired Helen Keller
      after she self-declared socialist
      pointing out
      her physical limitations
as if deafness & blindness
      entered her life
      as bodily defense against
      ideological transformation.
In 1919, Seattle workers sustained a citywide strike
      nonviolently,
      about which
      Anise wrote in labor's paper:
"The businessmen / Don't understand
      That sort of weapon...
      It is your SMILE
      That is upsetting
Their reliance / On Artillery, brother!"
      Not many read Anise's poems anymore.
      And Seattle now renowned
      for grunge rock & coffee shops.
In 1924, KKK Nights of Abhorrent Cloth
      masked America
      with over 4.5 million

white hoods.
In 1932, the Bonus Army came to D.C.
　　　imploring early depression-era payment
　　　of World War I bonuses
　　　already pledged:
twenty thousand vets were smacked back
　　　by McArthur, Eisenhower & Patton--the best
　　　military minds the U.S.
　　　could muster against its own.
Opposing the most elegant thuggery
　　　big business could buy,
　　　1.5 million U.S. unionists nonetheless
　　　went on strike 1934.
Since then wars have been fought--
　　　wars have been stopped.
　　　MLK's birthday declared a holiday--
　　　his radical democratic legacy quietly ignored.
Developing World materials and misery
　　　prop up the western wardrobe
　　　yet laughter & music become
　　　more internationalized than ever.
Despair/Desire, sorrow/hope, stenotopic/
　　　eurytopic--old stories witnessed
　　　in new ways. What is history
　　　if not a bit of wishful thinking?

KUSAL DHANANJAYA KURUVITAGE *(Sri Lanka)*

කුණාටුව
අවසන් විය
ජනෙල් වීදුරුවේ ඇස් අලවාගෙන
මැස්සෙකුයි මිනිසෙකුයි
ඔවුන් දෙදෙන
ස්කයික්‍රේපරයේ
මේ ජනෙල් කවුළුවෙන්
බොහෝ විනාශයන් දෙස බලා සිට ඇත
මේ තුනී වීදුරුව
ඔවුන්ට ලෝකය දක්වන'තර
සියල්ලෙන් ඈත් කරවන'යුරු
මේ තුනී වීදුරුව
චීන මහාප්‍රාකාරය තරම්
ශක්තිමත් යැයි සිතන්නා මෙනි
වීදුරු ගෙවල්වල වසන මිනිසුනි
තොප වීදුරු මත වසන
මැස්සන්ගෙන් වෙනස් වෙන්නේ කොහොම ද?
සියලු අසාධාරණයන්ට එරෙහිව
සියලු අයුක්තීන්ට එරෙහිව
අරගලය ඇවිලී ඇත මහමග
ඔහේ බලා හිඳී
ජනෙල් වීදුරුවේ ඇස් අලවාගෙන
මැස්සෙකුයි මිනිසෙකුයි

-කුසල් ධනංජය කුරුවිටගේ
[Kusal Dhananjaya Kuruvitage]

KUSAL DHANANJAYA KURUVITAGE *(Sri Lanka)*

UNTITLED

The storm ended.
Their eyes pasted
On the window-glass
Is a man and a fly.
Both of them have witnessed
Much ruination through this
Window of the skyscraper.
This thin glass has
Shown them the world outside
But the way it distances them
From the outside world,
This thin glass,
As though they believe
It were as strong as
the great wall of China!
You who live in glass houses
Tell me, how are you different
From a fly
The Uprising is aflame
On the streets,
Rising against inequity
Marching against injustice
But they stare vacantly from their window
Their eyes pasted on the glass,
A man and a fly.

(Translated from Sinhala by Vivimarie VanderPoorten)

D.L. LANG

WE MUST PICK UP THE PIECES

We must pick up the pieces
of the dreams our ancestors left behind
when they fought to change the world.

We must pick up the pieces
of love and carry them in our hearts,
so that it may spread to all humanity.

We must pick up the pieces
of this broken world and reassemble it
into a mosaic of great beauty.

We must pick up the pieces
of work unfinished and carry forth the vision
that things will change for the better.

We must pick up the pieces of this union,
rising up proudly together for as long as it takes,
so that humanity is assured a future
greater than anything we have ever seen.

GENNY LIM

PREMONITION

Those years blown
Like scattered leaves
In tumbling arpeggios
Flashing in the thrumming fingers of flames
Beating in the frozen harp of Black Angels
Old lovers faces framed in the amber of time
Trapped in the hollow breath
Of someone else's dreams
Someone else's myth of Eden
Languishing in the blues of misconception
Guilty as charged
With your insatiable will and spirit
The stones of memory don't lie
They archive the ruins of years
Whittled away by longing and
The unmitigated desire to
Summon in holy form
Love, with unfettered songs
Only the flowers can hear

MARK LIPMAN

A POEM I DIDN'T WRITE

There's a poem I didn't write
about train derailments
and banks collapsing
tumbling over like a bridge
with rusted pylons that fell
right into our drinking water
because I didn't know
whether I should call it
he or she.

There's a poem I didn't write
about world peace
about the chance we had
when the walls of an apartheid state
came down, because it never did,
it just went higher,
as we marched in the streets
for more missile sales for peace.

There's a poem I didn't write
about another mass shooting
encouraged by politicians
blaming the uterus
for the collapse of civilization,
while we cheered on drone strikes
as a kinder, gentler way
to steal the world's resources.

There's a poem I didn't write
about a dog gnawing
on a child's arm

while the cop kept repeating
"Stop resisting," for the cameras,
as I came to realize
that cats are better
for the simple fact
that they never worked
for the police.

There's a poem I didn't write
for an honest politician,
because looking left and right,
I just couldn't find one,
whether the excuse was told
through willful ignorance
or an outright lie,
in the end it made no difference,
the poor still died on the streets.

There's a poem I didn't write
about the day we finally woke up
and realized that other poor people,
regardless of where they were born,
are not our enemies,
that the billionaires
and their cronies
were the only ones
that felt our rage.

I didn't write that poem,
but I tell you,
my pen is ready.

ANGELINA LLONGUERAS　　*(Catalunya)*

FONTS

Ves a les fonts allà on ragen
ones de grans aventures,
en la quietud de les platges,
sota la llum de la lluna,
pren els camins que voregen
els camps de les altes dunes,
i no deixis mai que et vencin
els sotracs de la fortuna.

Ara respira la vida,
fent pauses com glopets d'aigua,
inspira i mira la imatge,
exhala tota la onada,
tot en la precisa mida,
la que el teu cos et demana.
No deixis res en els marges,
l'amor com una febrada.

I mentre et quedaran forces
contactaràs el que estimes
riuràs el vi de la vida,
viuràs la llum i la carn.
Fora les mentides mortes,
fora les converses llises,
que et difamin et fa forta,
et mouen altres afanys.

ANGELINA LLONGUERAS   *(Catalunya)*

SOURCES

Go to the sources where waves
of great adventure are born,
in the quiet of the beaches
under the moonlight
take the paths that surround
the fields of the high dunes,
don't ever let yourself be vanquished
by the ups and downs of fortune.

Now, breathe life,
pausing, like taking sips of water.
Inhale and look at the image,
exhale the whole wave,
everything in the right measure
the one your body demands.
Don't forget anything in the margins.
Love like a fever.

And while your strength remains
you will contact what you love,
you will laugh the wine of life
you will live the light and the flesh.
Down with the deadly lies!
Down with the flat chats!
Being defamed makes you strong.
You are moved by other desires.

(Translated from Catalan by the author)

OSCAR LOCATELLI   *(Italia)*

VERSI E CAREZZE

Voglio provare ancora
a credere che la cultura
(la poesia e la carezza)
e che la musica
(blues della bellezza)
salveranno questa
portaerei in fiamme.

Voglio sostituire
il nostro cuore di plastica
con uno di carta
ma di carta forte e resistente:
e sopra ci voglio solo
versi, note e respiro.

OSCAR LOCATELLI   *(Italy)*

VERSES AND CARESSES

I want to try again
to believe that culture
(poetry and caressing)
and that the music
(blues of beauty)
will save this
burning aircraft carrier.

I want to replace
our plastic heart
with one made of paper
but of strong, durable paper:
and on it I want only
verses, notes and breath.

(Translated from Italian by the author)

ANNA LOMBARDO   *(Italy)*

THE SONG OF COLOURED HOUSES

Red cuts and deep
In the clayey earth

Free diving in the sea
Harping with fresh trees

Down here talking about books
hearing voices of love, we saw the new world

Shut up, little soldier, don't be afraid
We carry poems not weapons

We will never sell our soul
To destroy this land

Once a poet wrote: "come and hang
your weapons to the branches of our rhymes" *

And now we tell you that you must too
Before it's too late

Please, abandon the masters of warfare
let them sing their bloody songs but alone

Breathe with us, disobey for peace
can't you see, war is not your skin

*   *The Albanian poet Ismail Kadarè*

ZIGI LOWENBERG

MUCH BITTER WITH THE SWEET

it really is too much. this world, now. maybe always. cycles of pause where you snatch breath and notice Beauty separate from excruciating horror. the *maror*. delicious liberation follows bitter herb, stories told every spring. the enslaved resist, clamor for justice, escape *mitzrayim*—that narrow place. *bitter with the sweet*.

you cower from muchness now, its unrelenting demand. how deep and thick the morass, roots impacted. pray to stay alive this one more night through sirens, helicopters, rubber bullets, tear gas. the world over, this is the lethal familiar. As if an occupied curfew can soothe with its coarse burlap uniform of war.

the artists carry you through. lifted in their arms like a baby in a basket saved from swift river, tossed softly your adolescent angst, nourished to buoyant.

milk rinse your eyes, gather honey and drop to any patch of earth. brush your skin on the surface of buds, verdant shoots, dew of renewal.

okay move along, fold your soapbox. mic in hand, mostly never a gun, but a hammer

(a wallet, phone) a bell, a song wrung with sweat.

while *Imagine …* plays your internal boombox

KIRK LUMPKIN

RUN OVER

*particularly for the women and girls of this country
and in protest of the Supreme Court conservative
super majority of Roberts, Thomas, Alito, Gorsuch,
Kavanaugh, and Barrett*

In their black robes
they seem more like priests
from some ancient cult
that cut out the hearts of virgin girls
while they were still beating
or burned to death
those they called witches

but, the image of their deliberative work
that arises for me
is them in formal black attire
at a vulture banquet
on a pregnant roadkill deer
squawking, flapping their feathers,
splattering blood,
pecking out her eye balls,
tearing out pieces of flesh and organs,
mining the cavity beneath her ribs
including the fawn fetus
as they eviscerate
our civil liberties and democracy.

Though my image of the court's majority
isn't a tightly constructed analogy
it does carry at least a little
of the feelings appropriate
to the multiple traumas of unwanted children
and the snowballing plague of over population;
to the pain, fear, frustration, and anger,
over another attempt

to take away her autonomy
over her own body—
our mothers, sisters, lovers, wives, daughters, aunts, nieces,
                                                    friends

all thrown under the bus
along with their
wild natural freedom
and cultured intelligence.

Unfortunately my image
also seems to demonize
vultures
who no being will ever need
to beg for mercy
for they only feed
on the already
thoroughly dead and rotting
that they find by smell
while these so called "justices"
are all over
her living body
no matter how young or old.

If only, if only, if only
a powerful feminine wave
could slap this
black robed posse
of sanctified vigilantes
back into place
and make them remember
that true justice
must be balanced
with mercy, oh mercy
we all need mercy,
sometimes.

BIPLAB MAJEE   *(India)*

মিথ অব সিসিফাস
বিপ্লব মাজী

আমাদের অনেক জন্ম অনেক মৃত্যু,
জন্ম মৃত্যু নিয়ে আর কিছুই ভাবি না,
যারা যায়, চিরদিনের মতো চলে যায়,
কোনদিনই আর এ গ্রহে ফিরে আসে না

স্মৃতি তর্পণে আমরা মাঝে মাঝে
তাদের কথা ভাবি,
--তারা কেন এসেছিল ?
--কেন বেঁচেছিল?
এই নিয়ে সাতপাঁচ ভাবি ।

আমাদের অনেক জন্ম অনেক মৃত্যু,
নক্ষত্রে নীহারিকায় আকাশে আকাশে
কোন অদৃশ্য শিল্পী
কেন এঁকে রেখে গেছেন?
কেউই জানি না।

অন্তহীন পথ হাঁটি...
পথ আর ফুরোয় না, পথের আর শেষ নেই,
চোখের সামনে ভেসে ওঠন সিসিফাস,
বুকে বাঁধা পাথর পাহাড়ে উঠছি আর নামছি..

BIPLAB MAJEE   *(India)*

MYTH OF SISYPHUS

We pass through many births and deaths.
I do not think of birth and death any more
Those who left they left forever
They will never come back to this planet

We remember them sometimes
While offering water to them --
Why did they come? --
Why did they live ?
We think this and that.

We pass through many births and deaths.
Nobody knows
Why an invisible artist drew
In the stars nebula and sky.

We walk through the endless path...
The road does not end,
the road has no end,
Sisyphus appeared before the eyes,
We go up and down the hill
with a stone tied to our chest.

(Translated from Bengali by the author)

这个世界的公民
—写给杰克赫•赫希曼

吉狄马加

你告诉我
你是一个行走在世界的人。

你的祖先
从乌克兰到意大利,
从蓝色的大海
到人潮涌动的纽约。
这并不是犹太人的宿命
但革命、自由与平等
却牵动着你家族的
不可更改的基因。

为诗而活着,或许
就是你存在的理由。
你是真正的知识分子
却一直游走在社会的边缘,
在那个反战,争取个人的权利
左翼的标语流动于街头的时代
你的狂热预言了未来的生活,
二十世纪有关身份的各种标签
都不适用于你无拘无束的个性。
在旧金山的街道上
你高大的身影弯曲着
在为那些普通的民众朗诵,

114

JIDI MAJIA   *(China)*

CITIZEN OF THE WORLD
For Jack Hirschman

You told me
you are a person who walks in the world.

Your ancestors
went from Ukraine to Italy,
from the blue sea
to New York with its surging crowds.
This wasn't actually the fate of the Jews,
but revolution, freedom, and equality
affected your family's immutable genes.

Living for poetry was perhaps
your raison d'etre.
You were a true intellectual
yet you always wandered on the fringes of society.
In the age of opposing war, fighting for individual freedom,
when left-wing slogans flowed on the streets,
your enthusiasm foretold your future life:
No Twentieth Century labels related to identity
would fit your unfettered personality.
On the streets of San Francisco,
your tall figure was bent,
reciting poems for common people;
the poems in your throat passed through solid skyscrapers,
storm-like sea waves beating against
every window of dried up souls.
This city's streetlamps knew you
just as you were familiar with the unfamiliar eyes
and the homeless whose names aren't known.

喉咙里的诗歌穿过了立体的高楼
海浪一般的风暴在拍打
每一扇灵魂干涸的窗户。
这个城市的路灯认识你
就如同你熟悉那些陌生的眼睛
说不出名字的流浪者。
因为你为自己确定的角色
那些无聊的评论家也很难
把你看成是无产者的诗人,
不过可以肯定你的思想和写作
却始终与穷人的命运连在一起。
当你喝醉的时候,老泪纵横
你的歌声饱含着对人类的爱。

不是你一个人在怀疑
人类为获得进步所付出的代价
到底有多大的价值?
人性中的恶从未远离过我们,
从叙利亚、阿富汗以及被
炮火覆盖的任何一个家园,
儿童的眼睛里布满了
这个所谓文明时代的恐惧。
你期待着马雅可夫斯基的复活,
相信他能跨过死亡的区域
在未来的某一天如期而至,
我们已经有好长时间
再没产生这样的英雄,
没有血性和理想的诗人

Because you defined your own role,
it was difficult for those mundane critics
to see you as a proletarian poet,
 but it is certain that your thinking and writing
were always linked to the fate of the poor.
When you were tipsy, tears coursed down your aged face,
your singing filled with love for humanity.

You were not alone in feeling skeptical
about the price humanity has paid for progress;
how valuable is it?
Evil in human nature has never left us;
from Syria to Afghanistan,
and any homeland covered in artillery fire,
children's eyes are filled with fear in this so-called civilized age.
You looked forward to Mayakovsky's reincarnation.
believing he would cross over death's realm
and arrive as expected someday in the future.
It has been so long
since we produced a hero like that.
Poets without courage and ideals
won't bring fortune to the people,
and the masses who move forward silently
long for a torch in the darkness.

Using a cane,
you went many places in the world,
from Russia to Haiti, from Colombia
to the Africa of the balafon,
from the star-filled countries in Eurasia,
to the East that is the East,
the countries imagined by the West.

不会给他的人民带来幸运，
而默然前行的大众
渴望的却是黑暗中的火炬。

你拄着拐杖
去过这个世界许多地方，
从俄罗斯到海地，从哥伦比亚
到巴拉丰琴的非洲，
从欧亚大陆上那些星落棋布的国家
到东方即东方
那些被西方想象过的国度。
你握过不同肤色的手
嘴里说得最多的一句话
就是要和平，不要暴力和战争。

你告诉过我
你是一个行走在世界的人。
而今天你留下的座位
却永远的空在了那里。
我不知道还会有多久
在我们中间才能涌现一位
这样富有热情与感染力
并充满传奇的世界公民。

You held hands with different skin colors,
and the sentence you uttered most
was that you wanted peace not war.

You told me
you were a person who walked in the world.
And today the seat you've left
will forever be vacant.
I do not know how long it will be
before there will be someone among us again
who is such a passionate, inspirational,
legendary citizen of the world.

(Translated from Chinese by Jami Proctor-Xu)

ELIZABETH MARINO

RAID

On vacation in Mexico

sleepy oceanfront town,

chilies and brine

white walls, dusty floors

a covered market.

A blast of light//

Three men charge in

Searching and firing

black and green turtlenecks

pulled up.

I drop down into an alcove's crevice,

wall meets floor.

A glimpse of a mean white face, then eyes

drop, as he glances past me.

Three bloodless bodies left behind.//

Through the door, left open

see their white van speed away.

They did not find you.

You were not there.

I tell no one of that face.//

"The police have found no suspects."

"The police have found no suspects."//

Back in our room

it is time to go. Now.

I turn and wake

tightly wrapped in your living arms

the cat nuzzling my nose.   ###

maybe the sun...

Oscar Locatelli

ÁNGEL L. MARTÍNEZ

PEACE SIGN

Peace sign:
Is it something that you sign with your hands
or make with your hands?
It is both and it is more
When you write poetry and songs
dedicated to a better world
while showing the road to it
It is when a mother
takes care of a child, many children
As we recall remembrance of motherhood
It is when you go out to save Earth
save life on it by a way, a movement saying:
We can build
We can plant the gardens
We can build the farms
We can run trains that carry food
to those who are hungry
When we say "peace sign,"
we talk about ending the poverty
that prevents peace
For as long as one person is hungry
or without a home or crying out for freedom
We still have the long road to go
to make that peace possible

ALBERTO MASALA   *(Italia)*

QUESTA POESIA CHE CADE
per i migranti morti nel mar Mediterraneo

Questa poesia che cade
rimbalza e si rialza
e ti ricade addosso
sulle spalle e le orecchie
ancora
la sto dicendo
e non so come inizia
perché questa poesia
è proprio come noi
iniziati per caso ad una vita
in questo mondo o un altro
così vitale ma
così vitale da farci dubitare
che ne siamo all'altezza
e quando muore
in questo corpo o un altro
la vediamo morire
in questi versi o in altri
la vediamo affogare
in questo fiume o un altro
in questa notte o un'altra
in questo sogno
dove non si sta bene
perché sento di essere osservato.

Così questa poesia
vive al mio posto
in questo corpo o un altro
in una lotta con la propria assenza
che si ripete uguale
e che ricorda
la stessa solitudine dell'arte.

ALBERTO MASALA *(Italy)*

THIS POEM THAT FALLS
> *for migrants who died in the Mediterranean Sea*

This poem that falls
bounces and gets up
and it falls on you
on the shoulders and ears
again
I'm telling it
and I don't know how it starts
because this poem
is just like us
initiated by chance into a life
in this world or another
so vital but
so vital as to make us doubt
that we are up to it
and when it dies
in this body or another
we see it die
in these verses or in other
we see it drown
in this river or another
in this night or another
in this dream
where things are not alright
because I feel like I'm being watched.

So this poem
lives in my place
in this body or another
in a struggle with its own absence
that is repeated equally
and that calls to mind
the same loneliness of art.

Così come l'amore
anche l'aria riempie le fessure
perché capisce istintivamente
le architetture intorno.
Anche la morte riempie le fessure
quando discende a prendersi la vita.
E la vita ricopre quel che resta.

Ma è un'altra vita.

Noi siamo in trappola
in una confortante gravità.
Un oceano di vita
potrebbe soffocarci facilmente.
Per poterlo affrontare
in questo nostro tempo senza uscita
duro da pronunciare
preferisco una *musica* più dura
della pacata musica di un libro
dove talvolta brucia e anche trabocca
la rivolta ma sempre così breve
che alla fine serpeggia agonizzante
davanti alla ragione
che impone la sua legge di realtà
e quando preme affonda nella carne
e una ferita chiara
attraversa la carne come artiglio
lasciando questo segno di chiarezza
e ci presenta tutti questi morti.

Forse questa poesia
può incrostare di ruggine le sbarre
per credere che forse
si romperanno.
Ho detto forse. Ancora
non ne siamo sicuri.

Just like love
Air, too, fills the cracks
because it instinctively understands
the architectures around them.
Even death fills the cracks
when it descends to take life.
And life covers what's left.

But that's another life.

We are trapped
in a comforting gravity.
An ocean of life
could easily suffocate us.
To be able to face it
in this time of ours with no way out
hard to pronounce
I prefer music that's harder
than the quiet music of a book
where sometimes revolt burns and even overflows
but always so short
which eventually meanders agonizing
in front of reason
which imposes its law of reality
and when it presses and sinks into the flesh
and a clear wound
cuts through the flesh like a claw
leaving this sign of clarity
and presents us with all these deaths.

Perhaps this poem
can encrust the bars with rust
to believe that maybe they will break.
I said maybe.
We're not sure yet.

Forse siamo l'essenza
di ogni rivolta morta in apparenza
il metodico battito del cuore
di rabbia antica e ruggine del tempo.
Ma non si può vedere ad occhio nudo.

Eccomi. Sono qui.
Ancora sul bordo del mio tempo
mentre prosegue il lutto
e qui non c'è nient'altro.
Hai visto quanti sono?
Non possiamo lasciarli alle parole.
Adesso vanno
oltre questa poesia
che s'interrompe qui.

È necessaria una follia migliore.

Perhaps we are the essence
of every dead revolt in appearance
the methodical beating of the heart
of ancient anger and rust of time.
But it cannot be seen with the naked eye.

Here I am. I'm here.
Still on the edge of my time
while mourning continues
and there's nothing else here.
Have you seen how many they are?
We can't leave them to words.
Now they go
beyond this poem
that stops here.

A better madness is needed.

(Translated from Italian by the author)

TOMMI AVICOLLI MECCA

I STAND WITH IMMIGRANTS

I stand with immigrants
border crossers
asylum seekers
I stand with refugees
dreamers
day laborers
I stand with my
southern Italian
grandparents
who were drawn
to the lamp
by the golden door
I stand with the
Statue of Liberty
and her promise to
the huddled masses
I stand with an America
that welcomes
the homeless
tempest-tost
not an America that puts
children and babies
in cages
or flies asylum seekers
to northern cities in
a game of gotcha
I stand with the America
of Emma Lazarus
not the America
of Ron DeSantis
or Donald Trump
or the MAGA masses
I stand with
an America that
remembers what
it stands for.

KAREN MELANDER-MAGOON

HUMAN LONGING

There is no metaphor for human longing
Though clouds may seem to touch the sky
Rivers pound inexorably towards the sea
Trees devour carbon dioxide
Greedily consuming our discarded air
To release life-giving oxygen
Yet even as the tides obey the moon
Sunflowers face the sun
Rain and snow pour down upon the earth
To fill again our lakes and seas
Distilled again into soft clouds
Floating in blue or steel-gray skies
Yet they are agents of the gears of seasons
Cyclical mechanics of timeless creation
They do not invent their purpose
Neither yearn to hold, protect or comfort
Just as galaxies spin pre-ordained in motions
They do not weep as stars explode
Or newborn planets disappear in black holes
Caves of deepest shadow
Absent lullabies
Even within the clanging of all time
There is no metaphor for human longing
No metaphor for love
That could suffice in all the universe
To tell its secrets

SARAH MENEFEE

HERE
      for Kaliphe Brown

'here in God's country
they can arrest you
for smiling

and you be dead
before they get you
to jail' he told his friend

'but depend on
the universe

that gave you your wits
to get you to where
you need to be'

TUREEDA MIKELL

PLAYIN IT COOL

Play it cool and dig all jive of
Class and race and what fed's say like
Church and state have two separate gates
Though Presidents swear in on the buy-bull
That states you're born broken babe
Say you're in the world but not of it?

Play it cool and dig all jive and
Beg forgiveness for being alive
Accept cost to live as contempt for existence
Blame Eve and Cain for hell's dominion
Illusion of inclusion sustains subtle bruising
Totalitarian trust secures delusions
Justice in just ice... judges the scheme
Degenerates telomeres nerves genes
Alternative facts redefine...first rule of war?
Confuse the mind ...you know

Play it cool and dig all jive
Watch American hegemony fail
Humanity's growth grow frail
Pawn nature's law in exchange for man's dog-ma
Schizophrenic bi polar tyrannies kill with impunity
Interrupt left right brain response-ability
Bank on stocks multitrillion pharma industries
Entertain affliction...fear and addiction
Police priest partner with dissed-ease
Promise the rapture will offer eternal peace
In the after life ... when you die
On your knees...heroically
Playin' it cool diggin' all the jive

Ignoring strange fruit on poplar trees
Smell more funerals than weddings
Child disappearances sex trafficking pornography
Houseless-nest organ and attention harvesting
Genocide G5, GMOs
Gain of function viruses
A.I. jabs with lipid nanos
m rna plastics craft spermicides
Cellular toxins wars without end ride
Suicide prevention and assistance websites
Is culture cancelling?
Why,
Play it cool and dig all this jive?

GAIL MITCHELL

WESTERN ADDITION MEMORIES

Listen………
Sometimes stories are like a whisper
of some old blues song you heard when you were a kid
and you tap your foot as soon as the first notes sound.

We are like birds who have the pattern of flight
Sewn in our minds
No need to remember
It's all laid out like a grid
And all you got to do is place yourself inside those
memories

Stories have a way of telling themselves
And you hear it in the voice of the teller
When Nana got here in the 40's
She stayed in a rooming house with Papa Al
The woman who owned the place
Said she didn't rent to Okies because they were nasty,
But they could have the room for the night

Nana needed to cook a meal
But the kitchen was so dirty…..she didn't know where to
                                                            start

So she cleaned that kitchen
And her and Papa Al had dinner and then went off to bed

Next morning, the hotel owner asked Nana
"Did you clean that kitchen? Nana said "Yes Maam!
The woman looked at Nana,
and told her what the rent was for the month.

The Western Addition was something back in those days
Oklahoma to Oakland on Southern Pacific
Then the Ferry to San Francisco
Everyone was happy just to be out of the South

Those old Majestic trains……..
Dreams traveled on those trains
The colored people were beautiful
Gold wrapped around teeth,
Big smiles, and working wherever they could
Papa Al worked at Southern Pacific

Nana got hired at a downtown hotel.
The old white man who hired her said
"Keep your mouth shut…..we don't hire colored people
But you can pass for Filipino if you don't talk."

She lasted a day,
That Okie whine was just a bit too much for him
She had pride and knew she could not sell herself short
Not even for some decent money.

Still she went to work and picked up some odd jobs
And finally found a job at the shipyard
And she sent for her daughter
And mama finished school at Girls High

ED MYCUE

DIPPING INTO THE WORD BANK

                                                a hop along the trail
waltzing strong through the de-materializing realizations
that abut and unite modern versions of trinket appraisals

my eyes begin to water but it isn't even tears that melt
it's my…."it can't be serious" muscle between the eyes
kicking up dust dirt gravel in the cavern of my sesame

because with so much beauty in the animals and bushes
with the emerald grasses clumping low near these lakes
why this disgusting transfiguration into so many broken

MAJID NAFICY *(Iran/USA)*

WE REMOVE OUR SCARVES

We remove our scarves
And use them to knit
A shroud for you.

No!
We will not weave
A hanging rope
With your turban.
You have already been
Dead for years.

We say: woman
We say: life
We say: freedom
And with the third shout
Our dead God collapses.

JERRY PENDERGAST

SHE'S SOWING SEEDS

Rows of grain and leafy plants
Of many
colors and sizes.

Her brows cooled
by a swift breeze
Tree branches bowing

next to a car
Agent scowls
in her direction

before entering, driving
back to his office.
Corporate logo on car door
In her field of vision.

Her neighbor,
former suitor
wipes brow
with hand that holds paper
that agent handed to him
She calculates the cost of a higher fence.

KATHY POWERS

SO MANY WORDS

They come to most forums:
So many words
Coiffed with hope intimations
Empty, ruling class promises.

Mass media blasts
Ghost messages in color
Insincere content
Meaningless, vacant, robotized smiles.

The ruling class steals human dreams,
Ignores real pleas from common angst,
Talks over essential needs,
Shuts down the cries from silent voices.

So many words
Fake understanding of obligations
Houseless, hungry, sick
Have no words, not even letters.

GREGORY POND

NEW ISM

when right nor left
quite represent
the people's concerns
or primary interests
and all we ever get is
left right back where we began
then we need better decisions
we need a brand new brand
we need a brand new ism
we need another other
to free us from the prison
that incarcerates us all
we need a social call
perhaps a call for social-ism
or some sort of government
which will lift us if we fall
too far into the schism
that has always existed
between the who is and the who isn't
one that throws a comforter
over those with less than
feeds the haven't eaten
beds the can't find sleep
and cares for the who needs healing
a commune, a communal
maybe a communistic tribunal
a mass community gathering
no slow or middle-of-the-road to fascism
but a world-wide revolution
a true planetarianism towards
a new humanitarianism

united to combat fear and greed
whose primary mission
is to house and feed
to spread no hatred or disease
and create a planet where we all will be
global promoters of love and peace

JAMI PROCTOR-XU

JUNIPER AND A LIFETIME OF WORDS

we walk in the arroyo beneath a tunnel of branches
i don't recognize   you say: juniper
and i walk between sunlight and sunlight through juniper
                                                    shade

when we stand beside a hundred years of white sycamore
and pray
you say: the living and the dead
and i rest my face on the white trunks' protrusions and
                                                    indentations

what can i give you
but a lifetime of words
an answer of not knowing when you say:
i miss you, i feel perplexed

when you walk before me, some of the rocks slip from
                                            their desert place
land on top of my feet
between red cloth and embroidered flowers
we reach the peak and you point out directions

north, south, names, east and west
i don't know where we are
in relation to here or anywhere else
together on a sunlit peak

april reaching toward a moonlit night
you fall into sleep telling a story,
a word is uttered, and i don't know if it's from the story
or from the dream you've fallen into, sleep, still talking

i ask you what it is, a horse running home
you awaken, startled
back into lamplight, under the quilt of handmade colors
what can i give you but a lifetime of words

juniper, sand, sunlight
a peak
where we see
through three languages, past direction

MARGARET RANDALL

OUR PROGRESS IS PLASTIC AND CEMENT

We measure and name our era
Holocene, drawing a line
beginning 11,700 years in the past
when that terrifying ice melted.
We call its surviving humans primitive,
imagine grunts, fire as prize, raw meat
and chance discoveries.

The experts stoke religious denial,
biblical time and progress
as superiority, describe a people
without history or written language
to bequeath us a narrative
of barely intelligent life, not a Shakespeare
or Mozart among them.

Atop Fajada Butte at the ceremony
that is Chaco Canyon,
we watch the dagger of light
split in perfect halves that spiral
carved on rock, note how each
Great House is aligned with a planet
and begin to unravel the lie.

Then we learn it's not only Chaco
but ancient sites across the globe
stone circles and mounds of earth
giving lie to our supremacy.
Ego of race and gender preceded by
that great ego of civilized man: a weight
we nurture shamelessly.

Studies not born of a single life
spent chasing the big prize
but centuries of observation.
Calendars that challenge the accuracy
of atomic time. Earth, sky,
and the human body stitched together
in a poetry of waiting.

Our progress is plastic and cement
clogging oceans, debris of all sorts
cluttering space. We turn our backs
on the energy of sun and wind,
rape the earth of its most vulnerable bounty,
invade and kill to stockpile a future
destroyed before it arrives.

Our academy praises such sophistication,
reaps billions in profit, while
the 300,000 inhabitants of tiny Vanuatu
ask if anyone cares their nation
is disappearing beneath a rising sea
in a future too close for comfort
or solution.

We were here, those ancestral voices
tell us, *but you didn't listen,
couldn't hear our stories,
honor our knowledge or the rhythm
of a wisdom that doesn't fit
this conviction you sustain
with your entitlement.*

GABRIEL ROSENSTOCK   *(Ireland)*

WAR AND PEACE IS A BILINGUAL TANKA
(5-7-5-7-7 syllables)
> *In Irish and English*
> *in response to artwork by Karl Wiener.*

cogadh is síocháin
cén gháir is airde amuigh
síocháin is cogadh
    ceabairé cam crólinnteach
    gan chríoch: cogadh is síocháin

war and peace: war! peace!
who is it shouts the loudest
war and peace: peace! war!
    grisly gruesome cabaret
    no end in sight: war and peace

Karl Wiener

SANDRO SARDELLA   *(Italia)*

DRIPPING DISCANTO
> *(a Jack Hirschman)*

1

Nella Storia il mare delle storie sovraccarico di
                    elmi spade e mitragliatrici
i libri sono muti   nel naufragare
              cadaveri euforici
                        parlano ai muri
il poeta americano sgrana centinaia di Arcani
canti epici sapienti furenti   sulla polvere
luccicante velenosa del sistema capitalistico
con il dito leggere e scrivere pensieri in fuga
              la scrittura si raccorda al cielo
s'impasta   di terraacquafuoco
ma la parola masticata riverbera la durezza di
                    Dei muscolosi e ladri

2

Nell'andirivieni del tempo   le gabbie
nella deriva dei riflessi   le ipocrisie
gli squilibri   le bugie
la gente curiosa inebetita ripulisce le tombe
                    di una memoria bruciata
i lamenti alla Coltrane di un sax sopra la notte
a occidente   la pianura dentro impallidisce
        su cieli mediorientali severi e spogli
e i nomi sono guerra e i corpi sono fame
di un navigare   per non smettere
ancora nomi   ancora corpi   ancora parole
perle morte   ambulanti   da masticare
tra il gelo di una intollerabile   indifferenza

SANDRO SARDELLA   *(Italy)*

DRIPPING DESCANT
                 (to Jack Hirschman)
1
Through History the sea of stories overloaded with
                  helmets swords machineguns
books are silent   in the shipwreck
         euphoric corpses
                  talk to walls
the american poet shells out hundreds of Arcanes
sagely raging   epic chants   on the
shimmering poisonous dust of the capitalist system
reading and writing with a finger fleeting thoughts
                  writing connects with the sky
blends   with earthwaterfire
but the chewed word reverberates the hardness of
                  muscular thieving Gods

2
In the coming and going of time   the cages
in the drifting of reflections   the hypocrisies
the imbalances   the lies
dopey busybodies clean out   the graves
of a burnt memory
the Coltrane laments of a sax over the night
in the west   the plains within turn pale
         on middle eastern skies   stern and bare
and   the names are war   and   the bodies are hunger
for navigation   never to stop
more names   more bodies   more words
dead pearls   wandering   to be chewed
in the chill of an intolerable   indifference

3

Pietre e vento squarci d'indecente bellezza
un fiore o una scarpa e   camminare
nei cimiteri del cuore danzando
nei cristalli del tempo annusa
le mie polveri sottili   nel fuoco delle banche
appartengo al popolo nel nome del pane
                                    senza padroni
i muri di Tunisi di Gerusalemme   di Odessa
con colori scritti   resistono
intralciano   i loro piani di guerra
suona tamburo   il vento fruga
                    dentro i capelli
nella piazza   aquiloni
tra sangue   bruciato   pestato
già spuntano i primi fili d'erba

4

Il bianco e il nero   è silenzio
scoprirsi nella neve   di aprile
con baci sulla bocca   sfacciati incantevoli
così violentemente   dolci
dove la guerra   non ha   un volto di donna
le mani meravigliose   oltre le macerie
lo scavo dentro   lo sguardo riconciliante
nutrito di visione sugli inganni sugli errori
mitici angeli delle discariche incidono
dopo l'erosione degli anni con l'inchiostro
una linea linea rossa   onda rabbia sabbia

3
Stones and wind   gashes of indecent beauty
a flower or a shoe and   walking
in the graveyards of the heartdancing
in the crystals of time smell
my fine particulates   in the pyre of banks
I belong to the people in the name of bread
                                        no masters
the walls of Tunis   Jerusalem   Odessa
in written colors   resist
thwart   their war plans
drum roll   the wind rummages
                through the hair
in the square   kites
in blood   burnt   trampled
the first blades of grass already sprout

4
The black and white is   silence
discovering oneself in   April's snow
with brazen enchanting   kisses on the mouth
so   violently   sweet
where war   has no   woman's face
splendid hands   beyond the wreckage
digging into   a conciliatory gaze
raised on visions   deceit mistakes
mythical angels   of landfills   etch
after the erosion of the ages in ink
a red   line line   wave sand fury

(Translated from Italian by Lapo Guzzini)

151

LUIS FELIPE SARMENTO   *(Portugal)*

I KNOW NOTHING ABOUT LOVE

Tell me about love. I will know nothing about love.
Perhaps a lamp in a dimly lit alley. Look, a butterfly stolen
from the collectors' aquarium. A cherry liqueur between
sheets... and then what? Perhaps the dawn colored by
Pollock's ghost. In Lisbon, of course. The accident at the
sunset of the unforeseen day. The big question is the
commonplace. The exercise of kitsch. What deflates in all
senses until the atomic shock. That interests me in this
unoccupied lucidity of everyday practice. The perspicuity
of acid and its emotional cocktail. I speak of singularities.
The fascinating universe of the unrepeatable. The love
without preexistence. In this suicidal leap against the
predictability of mimetic mating. I will say nothing about
love for a projection of the impossible. Until the touch-
moment of its existence. It is a closed page with no place
for the infection of the mob stripped of ideas and the
possibility of dreaming. This is how civilizations are
destroyed. Ours is already experiencing the stridency of
collapse. And they talk about love. This love as the result
of sinister impositions that the social world celebrates in
pornographic rituals. I associate acid with a velvety
brandy, avoiding the stairway of descent into the territory
of the living dead who speak of love with blood running
down their bones. I speak of a state so elevated that it
does not allow perversion. Yet in the eyes of the crowd
outraged by their ignorance I will be accused. I will know
nothing about love for a projection of the impossible; only

contact - without that Western reference of the degraded communion that is applauded by its protagonists and promoters - within the unique and unsubstituted combustion of a peaceful acid will elevate me to the nirvana of love without any manual for future incidences. I will not know how to say anything about love. In the detachment of that deliciously viscous molasses, without the penumbra of fear and shame, the gesture in the slow wave without the fear of time, between the body and the body of emptiness, the suspension of the mouth in the paralysis of a primordial scenario and in the same and intimate second the density of nectar in the absence of gravity of the immeasurable and unspeakable pleasure. I can say nothing about love. Nothing, lis love.

JOANNA SCANDIFFIO

ON A MONDAY AFTERNOON

in front of the Russian Embassy
a cyclist saw a man playing his cello
he stopped   the way a farmer stops
in the middle of his day to listen
   to light rain   the way a doctor takes a pulse
   a musician holds his bow in one hand and with the other
   steadies his instrument
   when the cyclist asked the musician, *Are you Yo-Yo Ma?*
   he replied, *Yes. Everyone has to do something.*

NINA SERRANO

FREE DUMP DAY

What an adventure!
We pulled out of the driveway
with the car stuffed
with all the boxes and bags
that were piled up in the garage
Boxes still unpacked from our move-in six years ago
and huge black plastic bags
full of unwanted give a ways and old clothes
and a discreet bag of electronic waste that just didn't
                                            work any more
The little car was packed in tight
with just enough room for us to sit in front
It was easy to spot the others en route
Pickup trucks filled to the brim
with old toys bicycles car parts and what not
Teams of people waving us in
indicating where we should go
You didn't have to get out of your car
There were more teams of people showing you
where to unload your loads
What a mobilization of people, equipment dumpsters
                                            and trucks
All about too much stuff
That doesn't even count
that most of our neighbors
have to park on the street
because their garages are full of stuff
Stuff is stuffing our lives
All along the highway sides
more storage units are being built

to put all the stuff in
We are choking on stuff
while others do without even a home
Free dump day helps free us of our societal shame!

KIM SHUCK

TO BEGIN POSITIVE CHANGE

Women's health care
Potentially a capitol offence
Maybe
We can't save our own lives
History
Subject to heavy-handed cosmetic surgery
Results
Poorly stitched
Scar tissue a
Message carried as we have
Carried others for
Better than two centuries
Some can read them
Some can
Run fingertips over the pulled and
Faked surface of this
Experiment an
Experiment a thing we are meant to learn from the
Most extreme truth that we can
Speak to power as we meet its
Eye
Smile and
Step right out of what it thinks is
Our lane

DINO SIOTIS *(Greece)*

ΜΑΥΡΕΣ ΤΡΥΠΕΣ

Ν' αρχίσουμε κι εμείς να φτιάχνουμε μαύρες
τρύπες να παραχώνουμε τα μαύρα κουτιά των
αεροπορικών και των άλλων ατυχημάτων του

πλανητικού μας πολιτισμού, να μη μάθει
ποτέ κανείς τίποτα απ' όσα έλαβαν χώρα όσο
ζούσαμε, ούτε για τους πολέμους, ούτε για την

πανδημία, ούτε την οικολογική καταστροφή,
ούτε τις εξεγέρσεις των απελπισμένων, ούτε
για το προσφυγικό, το φασισμό, το ρατσισμό,

και την έλλειψη κριτικής σκέψης, άσε που δε
νομίζω να υπάρχει κάποιος που θα νοιαζόταν
πώς ήταν ο κόσμος το έτος 2022 μετά Χριστόν

DINO SIOTIS   *(Greece)*

BLACK HOLES

Let's start making black holes to
hide the black boxes of air crashes
and other accidents of our planetary

civilization, not to learn never anyone
anything that took place as long as we
fight, neither for the wars, nor for the

pandemic, nor the ecological disaster,
nor the uprisings of the desperate,
neither about refugees, fascism, racism,

nor the lack of critical thinking, never
mind if our fractured world cannot
accept a credit card of euphemism,

our mission to heal goes without saying,
our verses are becoming swords ready
to kneel anyone who blocks our way

(Translated from Greek by the author)

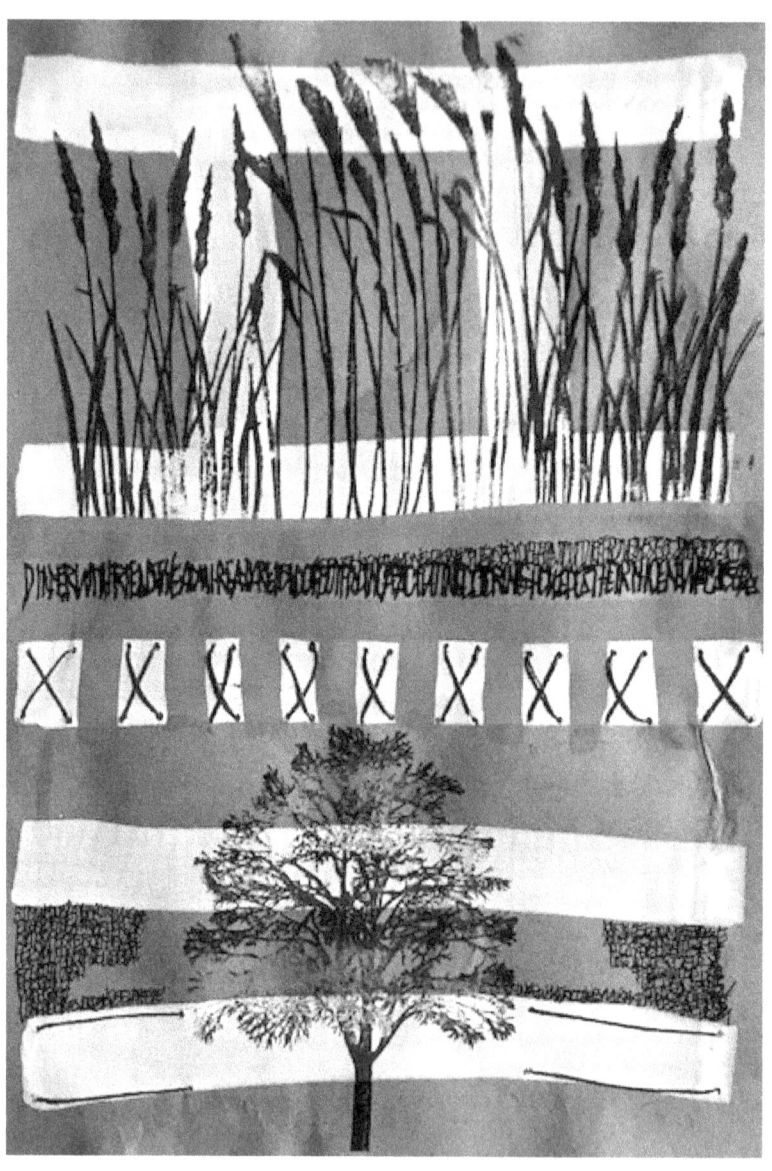

Barbara Byers

DOREEN STOCK

"BY THE ROAD TO THE CONTAGIOUS HOSPITAL"
after W.C.Williams

Or rather across the road from it,
amid those hills of the eternal variety, a community of
oaks pinning down the grassy slopes

lest they drift upward to become one with
their puffy overlords hanging down, shadowing them,
gently moving across their faces

What if it's the oaks who send us from their
rooty network consolation—that silence heard
in our white corridors of grief, despair, fear,
pain. What if it's consolation that heals

all who breathe in the contagious hospital
never suspecting that the forms they see out
the window are breathing with them, singing
with them in the silent language of all that is?

And *all along the road the* *upstanding, twiggy stuff of*
bushes
and small trees with dead, brown leaves under them
leafless vines— what if they are communicating
among the x-rays, the tubes of blood, the yards of
gauze and pounds of plaster saying simply, "stand
up, you can do it" to the frail, the weighted, the suddenly
dispossessed?

On the road to the contagious hospital today I could see

161

once more my own father in his last moment, breath
                                        leaving,
light leaving his eyes his profile relaxing against the trees,
the hills, the grass, in the dignity of his exit among them…

And what if the eyes seeking clouds find them filled
with the gentle rain of tears that can ease what's broken,
flown, undone?

MATTHEW TALEBI

OUTSIDE IN THE RADIANCE

Outside in the radiance of Sun rise.
Doves sitting on the satin day of your longing.
Singing to dawn of spring.
Joy and peace
Embrace essence of being

Trumpets roar.
Sun gets behind macabre clouds.
Big birds with scarlet beaks and claws
Sanguine flooding. deadly heavy metals
Enter the scene of surprise.
Lost lives replaced by bouquets of sobs

 Scarifying crystalline tears
Doves fly away sadly
 Windowpanes masked misty
To blind the truth of fatal tragedy

You fall frozen inside the four walls
 of   your sweet dreams and memories.

SARAH THILYKOU   *(Greece)*

ANCIENT ANGER

From the depths of the future
an ancient anger is rising

act one of history
I stand out and wonder
who was the assassin of my brother
the human voice replies to me
I

I
the ancient beast
I
in the dullness of the world
I
am not you yet

You
are standing in front of me

don't be afraid
sing to me
write to me
as humanly possible
be at last
a human
let me be

RAYMOND NAT TURNER

THE TENNESSEE THREE SPEAK IN WE

> "Alabama got me so upset,
> Tennessee made me lose my rest…"
> —Nina Simone, "Mississippi Goddamn"

I.
Cherokees "on the road again." Violently herded West.
Ethnically-cleansed on crimson Trail of Tears. Forcibly
moved off Tennessee homeland to
Oklahoma—Where land acknowledgment ain't enough…

II.
Lorraine Motel balcony; Audubon Ballroom; Mississippi
driveway; Chicago bedroom; UCLA lunchroom polling
places—Our leaders were voted out of office with lead
Ballots: swapping steel Lumumba for malleable Mobutu!

We were left standing on Duopoly corners harmonizing
$campaign/$election songs: "Yes, we can!" and "I feel
your Pain." Left praying to Pentagon parties of Long COVID
capitalism for depleted uranium, white phosphorus prosperity

Lightfoot-Drone Rangers remained…Bassackwards Strong-
arm Williams Thom-ass Clarence Tribesmen trained to lead
us in the treacherous 2/4 Dance—
Donkey dung-elephant excrement dance—Every 2-4 years

III.
The Tennessee Three speak in We—
from moribund bodies high on white powder in
Corporate crack pipes—
Apartheid state bodies of banana Republican rule

The Tennessee Three speak in We—

165

in NRA faces of gerrymanders coming
out of caves and fronting for Fat-cats—
Civil War hawks—quacking like lame ducks

The Tennessee Three speak in We—
to bought and bossed good ole boys—Volunteer
State puppets— Paymasters' hands up nazi asses,
Moving 2nd Amendment/Maximum profit mouths
The Tennessee Three speak in We—
to dog whistling faces of foghorn framers—
Ventriloquists called confederates—Or,
their more modern name: Fascists!

The Tennessee Three speak in We—
to whipping post politicians, rebel-yelling in
cat o' nine tails tongue—"Tantrum" tommyrot—
branding The Peoples' Needs: "Wanting attention!"

The Tennessee Three speak in We—
facing starred-barred,
water-hosed, dog-bitten Dixie—Hurricanes of
hardship—Awash with Stax waves of solidarity

The Tennessee Three speak in We—
Standing and delivering! Amplifying voices of ones once
Celebrated "Essential" in nightly pot and pan banging and
clanging concerts

The Tennessee Three speak in We—
Standing and delivering! Amplifying voices of shoe leather,
street heat, pavement politicians, rising in rippling waves of
Maladjusted millions… flicker of what democracy looks like??

Sandro Sardella

VIVIMARIE VANDERPOORTEN   *(Sri Lanka)*

Nandikadal *

In Jaffna
Young people
Are still writing poetry
About Nandikadal
They are writing about
Being born a girl
And dowries
And arranged marriages
But also about
Nandikadal
They are reading poetry
In Tamil and the passion
Bursts out of their lips
And eyes
They are writing about
Water crises
And death
And I who have written about
The war realize
I am illiterate
In war
And though I cannot understand
The language
I can hear the fury
And feel the fire
They have not outgrown
The pain
Like
we shouldn't outgrow
The memory

Before forgetting we need
To remember
This lagoon of lament
And the restless dead
that led us
There.
Young people
In Jaffna
Are still reciting poetry
About
Nandikadal

** Nandikadal lagoon was where the final battle of
the 30 year civil war in Sri Lanka was fought,
between Government troops and the Liberation
Tigers of Tamil Ealam (LTTE)*

DAVID VOLPENDESTA

FORBIDDEN PSALM TO A WORLD WITH A BROKEN SPINE
To the Poor

When the wealthy
look into the eyes of a crystal ball
they see themselves
making gigantic profits
off climate change.

A flash of lightening in a broken jar
is the earth falling from the sky,
with all the planets in the universe.

For some life is luxury, liquor, and pills,
not to mention mountains of money
to buy Rolls-Royces
while their chauffeurs
are paid minimum wage
and dress in second-hand clothes
while their bosses
buy fancy gold watches,
diamond rings, stocks and bonds,
and ten-thousand-dollar suits.
That is being successful.
That is why they were born.

Imperialism is the suicide of the soul
just like heroin
or better yet fentanyl
because it goes more quickly
to outer space
from where very few

will be coming down.

When rich people
think of money
before they fall asleep at night,
they don't think of starving children
who are begging for penny candy.

The snobby millionaires
tell those kids to get a job
and a change of clothes
and tell their parents
to quit living off welfare.

To the imperialist class
your heart is just a commodity,
just more flesh in a nuclear war.
Dominate the body.
Hunt down the soul.
This is the United States
where everything has a negotiable price!

There will come a time
when the eagle will chase the fox
up and down the valley
and the squirrel will find an acorn
in the tallest tree
and children will teach adults
about the wonders of the world
and the glories of light.
They will dance on the boundless air,
because children will find reality
behind the infinite illusions.
Yes, children will begin
to heal a fractured world!

CATHLEEN WILLIAMS

THE PAST HAS NOTHING FOR YOU

under the eaves
of the station
a storm of sparrows

waiting passengers
have deserted the trackside
the train has come &
gone

the blue, the faded blue
of the old door –

the millennials I know
fly by night like arrows
armed with revolutionary ideas

the past has nothing for you
except its beauty
except its destruction

D.A. "ROARSHOCK" WILSON

100 THOUSAND POMEGRANATES FOR PEACE

Now has come September
harvest mostly in
last radishes dug
from the ground
last green tomatoes
wrapped in paper
and stored in the pantry.

On the southside
of the house
the pomegranate-tree
droops beneath
the weight of fruit.

They grow
all through
a solitary summer
small green bulbs
to large red balls.

Out of the unexpected blue
cosmic transmissions on the social web
networks of dozens
of brilliant supportive poets
spatially dispersed around the planet.

I was contacted by Paul Jolly
one of the first poets I knew
back at last in old Berkeley
after decades away from poetry,
but now returned with his great sincerity.

In pleasing synchronicity
I had been thinking of Paul

173

a day before his contact.
Remembering the time
he approached me at school
and held forth two halves of
a pomegranate
myriad bright red seeds
gleaming, glistening
under high ceiling lights.

"We are the pomegranate."
He said laughing
and I laughed.
For us "we are the pomegranate"
became our catch phrase
a metaphor.

Harvest the pomegranates
before they bend the tree to breaking
two huge baskets
these will be good
until February.

Survive another perilous year!
Fingers crossed, nervous
spells and incantations
breath right
relieve stress
and whatever boosts immunity.

Dry California
waits for rains
to douse the parched land
knock down the wildfires
for a while.
In the United States
and other lands
fraudsters peddle "alternative facts"
confuse the gullible and uneducated

while war, pandemic disease
floods, fire, and famine
sicken and kill
100 thousands of people
and other creatures
around the world.
Yet dummkopfs
gather and march
from Berlin to Brazil
to way down in Texas.
Hell, no! We won't wear masks!
We will not vaccinate
Or be blinded by science!
Elections are a hoax!

But I declare
we are the pomegranate.
All of us, regardless of our vision
be it cloudy or clear
and if we are striking out
because we are so injured
so emotionally hurt
so fearful that we hit and hurt,
we can instead be forgiving
and love ourselves and others
we can reach out in love
to all the brilliant seeds
all the love radiating from souls
we can help and heal
all together now
love is all we need
and the pomegranates
growing again next year
and every year
let the seasons roll around
we are the pomegranate.

NELLIE WONG

BLUE

Blue Mind Day
masking, laughing
with the wind, no
herons in sight
blue of sky, growth
of sticky monkeyflowers
along the path, houses
across the water, mother bird with chicks, mewing
of gulls, seabirds.
Ships in wait,
patience tested,
cargo of automobile
and computer parts, toys, steel I-beams.
Blue marble centers
the view, tomorrow's
herons, the air
of summer, songs, stones and glass
surrounding poems
and we sing.

ERIC ALLEN YANKEE

BRICK WALLS

I've seen so many young people
sitting against a brick wall,
backpacks with holes,
shoes with soles flopping,
and desperate eyes searching.
no home in sight.
only wordless passerby,
passengers on the train
to a world without understanding.
just more brick walls,
and more young people
to blend in with the bricks.

LORENE ZAROU-ZOUZOUNIS   *(Palestine/USA)*

AWAKENINGS

Waking alarm shocks, ear rings,
heart tempos, breath doubles
Eyes feel weight of body fluid
Head heavy, a water-logged stump sinking
Torso pops up a vampire at dawn,
draining necks of the Fertile Crescent

Static-loaded, splintered subliminal messages,
biased censorship lodged
into brain's vacancy
One-liners, mindless cliches, military jargon frequencies
Sopped up into mushbrained gullible patriotic mobs

Seep out freedom tales, fantasies of saving the destitute (but
they were not)
News blues programmed horrors over and over and over
Noon, 2 pm, 4 pm, 6 pm, 8 pm, 10 pm, late night propaganda
my great-grandmother's grave dug up snaps my thoughts-
for a homicide autopsy-I wish and dream

Tears translucent, saliva dribbles
into my ear, muffling spread of death through ancient land,
alternating news-unfinished-dreams-nightmares-awakenings
Arise to a new day to white male war lord deceptions,
Western dictators and "deciders" of who to incinerate next
ethnic cleansing, blanket bombing decimating
towers of Babylon and springs of kings and queens

Masses put to sleep like sickly shuttlecocks with bird flu
while one female Secretary of State affirms it necessary
and perfectly okay for 5000 children to perish each month;
and she actually stopped calling on me for questions--the only
one in the room

not buying her bullshit while a mesmerized dazed audience
                                        cheered her
and stared me down like I was the terrorist war woman
I kept pressing her about years and years of sadistic sanctions
annihilating masses of children, not to mention starving millions
from US/UK criminal sanctions deemed productive, essential
And yet another female Secretary of State avowed "it was
                                worth it"—all the dead
in a jingoistic-precision-not-so-smart-bombing-campaign-of-
                                        liberation

Leave me where I am-blissfully warm under cover
without radio and tube false news barkers
imbedding brain wave maiming noises
brainwashing an-already-dumbed-down-flag-waving populace
                                (for the most part)
...that 911 revenge genocide in Iraq and Afghanistan is "mission
                                accomplished"
and flag draped silenced sons arrive—(many knew these two
                                        countries
were not to blame for 911 massacre)

Iraq's ancient Mesopotamia "smart" bombed
back to the dark ages to control oil fields for over consumption
and natural gas reserves we later find out undersea plan/route
Protect a so-called democracy in the Middle East was always
                                        in the
hidden war machine-agenda-masterplan,
and where are the other "sides" of this "Middle"?...
and by the way, the "Middle East Peace Talks," a fat lip service
                                and a trick

And then there was around these times
as years of attacks on Iraq and Afghanistan persisted,
Somalia starved, shriveled
The son of a priest ordered a genocide in Yugoslavia.
Palestinians were piled in internment camps,

179

urine-stained potato sacks over bashed heads upon arrest;
denied trials in a brutal iron fist occupation
of an indigenous race losing ground in historic Palestine

Go away, I'll sing me a love song
Tell me something good,
in the darkness of undercover,
in the tardiness of autumn sunrise
Soothing sun streaks, high-pitched chippers,
and a sweet voice from luscious lips,
finally awakens me
She kisses me to rising and daddy whistling
Transition of consciousness after a junk wave head rush
I slip into a daydreaming euphoric ecosphere,
where every child knows only love

Her timing of words, gestures
synchronize with need, want, sanguinity
Six dry, glazed eyes become one eye
Moist hands clutch, fitting perfectly
Her fingers held high like an Intifada poster child,
smiling wonderfully, she exclaims "peace"
I mimic her as I become her student
She continues "peace on Earth mommy," "I love you"
sucking her thumb, cuddling center
I stare into a 30's dresser mirror,
a single tear barely wets her forest thick hair,
for the truth I must reveal

*Written after the US/UK alliance attacked
and occupied Iraq in the 90's, revised-2023*

ANDRENA ZAWINSKY

BULLETS

Bullets,
their brassy caps
glinting golden in the dark
ammo tray tucked under
a student study desk,
more bullets in a bandolier
crisscrossing the chest, bullets
maneuvered across a screen
in slugs of anger and angst
in bullet launchers, landmines
of bullets, bullets of the slain
in a shooting game.

Bullets,
their powder packed cartridges
of panic and fear, hollow points
shattering identities, blasts
sounding in sleep, bullets
of grief from a spray hate.

Bullets
that silence at windows, on lawns,
on street corners, in schoolrooms,
supermarkets, factories, churches,
all turned altars of flowers,
candles, placards, and prayers,

while bullets
fill bank accounts
of makers and regulators

dodging bullets whistling by,
shells jingling in pockets
like loose change spent
in puddles of blood.

Bullets,
their full metal jackets
dug from the corpse
with its legacy of wounds,
bullets that pierced the flesh,
shattered the bone, riddled
the heart and all the wild in it,
depositing dreams
to urns and coffins
buried in holes in the dirt,
screams smothered,
breaths sealed.

BIOGRAPHICAL NOTES

TONY ALDORANDO's poems embrace his love for his Puerto Rican heritage and his empathy for humanity.

NAHID ARIA, an Afghan-American poet and artist residing in the Bay Area, created one of the graphics in this anthology

ADRIAN ARIAS is a poet, visual artist, and activist. He is the creator and curator of *Tarot in Pandemic and Revolution*, from Nomadic Press, 2022.

AYO AYOOLA-AMALE is a poet, artist, and Director of the Splendors of Dawn Poetry Foundation, in Nigeria. Her poems confront violence, racism, and the breakdown of the Yuma community.

MAHNAZ BADIHIAN, a poet and artist, has published many books in Farsi and English. Her recent collection of poems, *Ask the Wind*, was published by Vagabond in 2022. She runs, Mahmag.org.

LISBIT BAILEY 's most recent chapbook is *Horizon*. She co-edited the 2021 and 2022 RPB anthologies. Her poems are in This Wandering State, from caliballiance.org/; *Tarot in the Time of Pandemic and Revolution* from Nomadic Press, and *Third Rail*'s online incarnation at literatureandarts.com/.

KEMLYM TAN BAPPE is a poet and artist from Singapore who is a special education teacher in Arizona. She is the host of "Between the Lines," and presented at the Smithsonian Museum of American Art.

LYNNE BARNES is the author of *Falling into Flowers* (2017). Her work appears in *Poets11 Fog and Light: San Francisco through the Eyes of the Poets who Live Here and Light on the Walls of Life.*

VIRGINIA BARRETT is a poet, writer, artist, editor, and educator. Her six books of poetry include *Between Looking* (Finishing Line

Press) and *Crossing Haight—San Francisco poems* (Jambu Press).

ALESSANDRA BAVA is an Italian poet and translator of the poem of Marco Cinque. She is writing a biography of SF Poet Laureate emeritus Jack Hirschman.

BENGT BERG is a Swedish poet and activist who's published 40 books, mostly of poetry, which have been translated into many languages. He was a member of the Swedish Parliament from 2010-2014 representing the Left Party.

JUDITH AYN BERNHARD Is the author of the poetry collection, *Prisoners of Culture* and a book of short stories, *Marriages.* A former llanguage instructor, her literary translations and poems have appeared in numerous anthologies. She lives in San Francisco and teaches writing.

DANIEL BROOKS is a writer, poet, editor, and special education teacher. His work has appeared in the *Indianapolis Review, the Hawai'i Review, the People's Tribune,* and on Kallatumba Press

KRISTINA BROWN is a writer, painter, poet, and co-editor of this anthology. She often writes about what people will, and will not, do for love.

BARBARA BYERS is a mixed media artist, photographer, and educator, living in New Mexico. She is a long-time collaborator on many books with poet Margaret Randall, including *Stormclouds Like Unkept Promises*.

JIM BYRON created over 350 songs and released more than 20 albums between 2018 and 2020.

GIANCARLO CAMPAGNA lives in Santa Rosa. When he's not writing poetry or spending time with his family, he works at Safeway in the Deli Department.

JANET CANNON is the author of three chapbooks: *Day Laborers, The Last Night in New York,* and *Percipience*. She has read her poems all over the country in spoken word events.

ATEFEH CHARMAHALIAN is a poet, children's rights activist, and former Iranian Writers Association board member.

MARCO CINQUE writes, photographs, plays ethnic instruments, recites, publishes essays, poetry collections, and articles. He has published more than 30 books and has been translated into English, Spanish, Albanian, and French.

FRANCES COMBES is one of the most politically engaged poets in Paris and all of France. He is the coordinator of the World Poetry Movement for Europe, and the leader of a group of French poets, La Merle moqueur.

KITTY COSTELLO's collection Upon Waking: New & Selected Poems 1977-2017 gathers 40 years of her San Francisco writings. She is co-editor of the anthology *Muslim American Writers at Home: Stories, Essays & Poems of Identity, Diversity & Belonging,* helping to overturn Islamophobia.

ANITA ODENA CRUZ is a member of Hayward's B Street Writers Collective and Bay Area Poets Coalition. She won first place prizes for *Make a Living as a Poet* and *Edith,* and read at Jack Hirschman's Poets 11 for Bayview, SF.

ROMEO ALCALA CRUZ writes poetry in both English and Bicol (rawit dawit). He is the author of *Washing Rice and other Poems* and *Crossing the River from Memory to Forgetfulness.*

JOHN CURL is a co-editor of this anthology. His latest poetry collection is *Rainbow Weather: Poems for Environmental Healing* (Vagabond Books, 2022). He recorded his poetry for Voetica.com. His work can be found on www.johncurl.net

AMIT DAHIYABADSHAH is the author of *The Tiger Poet New and Selected Poems,* his 21st collection. He believes poetry will help "Change" not through great poets and great poetry, but more poets and more poetry, ie: the poetry of "We the People."

GARY S. DANIEL (NÈG GONBOLYEN) is a Haitian poet who writes under the pen name "Nèg Gonbolyen."

LUCILLE LANG DAY is the founder of Scarlet Tanager Books and a science and health educator. She has written or edited over 20 books and is a contributor to over 50 anthologies.

DIEGO DELEO came to the USA from Bari, Italy 70 years ago, when he was 17. His third book, *I'm Tempted to Write a Poem*, was published in 2021.

VIVIAN DEMUTH is an award-winning author of two ecological novels, *Bear War-den* (2015) *Eyes of the Forest* (2007), and a poetry book, *Fire Watcher* (2013). She has worked as a mountain fire lookout in the United States and Canada, where she hosted a poetry on the peaks event.

CAROL DENNEY is Berkeley cartoonist, poet, and musician. An award-winning lyricist, poet, guitarist, fiddler and concertina stylist, she was a founder of "Fiddlers for Peace," curator of the "Deep Poetry Project," and founder and editor of the *Pepper Spray Times.*

GERMAIN DROOGENBROODT has written 17 poetry books, published in 31 countries. He has received many international awards, is yearly invited to international poetry festivals, and was nominated in 2017 for the Nobel Prize of Literature.

CARLOS RAÚL DUFFLAR is a poet, playwright, peace activist and a member of the New York Revolutionary Poets Brigade. He is also a member of the Academy of American Poets and, as of September 2023, a New Generation Lifetime Beat Poet Laureate.

AGNETA FALK Is a poet, artist, and a member of the World Poetry Movement. She is preparing her third major volume of poetry for publication.

MAURO FFORTISSIMO is an Argentinian/Italian/American musician, painter, poet, and activist. Born in 1962, he moved to the US and the Bay Area in 1980.

MARK FISHBEIN graduated CCNY in 1971, attended the Sorbonne, has five books of poetry, and currently lives in Chicago. He is currently Chancellor of the Poetry Academy of

PGN-Poetry Global Network, hosting numerous workshops and events, including Planet Poetry 28.

MARCOS DE SOUSA FREITAS is a poet, engineer, and environmental and cultural activist. He lives in Brasilia and is the author of *In The Coming Afternoon.* He is the current president of the Academia de Letras do Brasil (ALB).

LUIS GARCÍA explores his ancestral roots through a myriad of visual and written artistic processes. There is a duality, a split in having been born into one culture (El Salvador) raised in another (U.S.), seen as immigrant, now as citizen. Dichotomy is a word that seems to best describe his arrival to this worldview; a worldview that has been in process his whole life.

RAFAEL JESÚS GONZÁLEZ, retired professor of Creative Writing & Literature and Mexican & Latin American Studies, was four times nominated for a Pushcart Prize, and was named the first Poet Laureate of Berkeley, California.
Visit http://rjgonzalez.blogspot.com

ART GOODTIMES, poet, basket weaver, and former Green party elected official in Colorado, served as Western Slope Poet Laureate and is currently poetry editor for fungimag.com and sagegreenjournal.org

EGON GÜNTHER lives as a poet and painter in Upper Bavaria.

LAPO GUZZINI is a San Francisco-based translator, editor, and arts agitator. He has translated the poem of Sandro Sardella in this issue, and is completing a book of Sardella's poetry.

KAMRUL HASSAN, a poet of the 1980s, has published 14 books of poems. Besides poetry, he writes short stories, travelogues and articles, and translates literary works in English into Bangla and vice-versa.

BILL HATCH is the editor of Badlands Journal and works on environmental issues in the San Joaquin Valley. He is also author and composer of *Shellburg Blues*, and translator of poems of Roque Dalton.

MARTIN HICKEL, child of the paradise which is the San Francisco Bay region has always wondered why more people don't open their eyes. He's been busy doing nothing and going nowhere for a while now and hopes to continue as long as possible.

JACK HIRSCHMAN, who completed his life work defending the planet and building socialism, was both an emeritus Poet Laureate of San Francisco and co-founder of the Revolutionary Poets Brigade.

BRUCE ISAACSON is a poet and publisher living in Las Vegas, Nevada. His Zeitgeist Press has published approximately 112 books.

SUSU JEFFREY grew up in the American Midwest on mashed potatoes and politics. Her first two books were about her Roma (Gypsy) ancestry, followed by collections about politics, love, water (*Mississippi Mother*, spoken word CD) and now trees.

ZIBA KARBASSI is a Tabriz poet from north-western Iran who has lived in the UK from an early age and is widely regarded as the leading Iranian poet living in exile. She has brought and opened a subject to poetry called Breath poetry.

ELIOT KATZ is the author of seven books of poetry, including *Love, War, Fire, Wind* and *Unlocking the Exits*, as well as *The Poetry and Politics of Allen Ginsberg*. He has worked for many years as an activist for peace and social-justice causes, including helping to create housing and food programs for homeless families in Central New Jersey. www.eliotkatzpoetry.com.

KUSAL DHANANJAYA KURUVITAGE studies Intention, Conservatism, and Thomism as student of faculty of law, Colombo university and Sri Lanka Law college.

D.L. LANG is an internationally published poet who served as poet laureate of Vallejo. Find her at poetryebook.com

GENNY LIM is the recipient of the PEN Oakland Lifetime Achievement Award. A former SFJazz Poet Laureate, her play, *Paper Angels*, has been produced internationally. She is coauthor of Island: *Poetry and History of Chinese Immigrants on Angel Island,* winner of the American Book Award.

MARK LIPMAN, founder of Vagabond press, the Culver City Book Festival and the Elba Poetry Festival, is author of more than twelve books, including *The Role of the Revolutionary Poet in Society*. His radio program, Poetry from Around the World, is on KPFK 90.7FM Los Angeles. Mark is currently traveling the world, building consciousness through the spoken word.

ANGELINA LLONGUERAS, born in Barcelona, is a Catalan actress, playwright, stage director, activist, poet, educator, interpreter, and researcher.

OSCAR LOCATELLI lives in Bergamo, Italy, where he is a redactor of a magazine of workers' writings, *Abiti/Lavoro.*

ANNA LOMBARDO, poet, free translator and cultural activist, lives in Venice and is the art director of the International Poetry Festival Palabra en el Mundo. Her recent poetry book is *Con candide mani* (2020). She recently translated Matt Sedillo's poetry book *Stolen Lives, Stolen Land* into Italian for Ensemble.

ZIGI LOWENBERG is a performance poet and co-leader of the jazzPoetry ensemble UpSurge! which has produced CDs under the name, *All Hands on Deck.*

KIRK LUMPKIN is a poet, performer, spoken word artist, lyricist, environmentalist, cultural worker, and event organizer. Author of two books of poetry, he lives in Mendocino with his wife on 80 acres of undeveloped land; his recent project is writing about poison oak.

BIPLAB MAJEE is a leading Bengali poet, writer, literary critic and translator. He has published 28 books of poem, 36 books of prose, and 16 books of translation.

JIDI MAJIA is a Yi-Nuosu poet born in 1961 in Sichuan. His book of poems *My First Love* won the National Poetry Prize of China. *The Dream of a Yi Native* won the fourth Literary Prize of China Minorities for poetry.

ELIZABETH MARINO is a Chicago-based RPB member, poet, educator, and performer. Her work has appeared in 20+ anthologies, as well as the full-length collection *Asylum* and two chapbooks.

ÁNGEL L. MARTÍNEZ is a poet, musician, peace activist, and a member of the New York City Revolutionary Poets Brigade. He plays bass guitar, guitar, and electronic effects.

ALBERTO MASALA. A poet and a performer, Masala was born in Sardinia in 1950. He is a "today's artist with roots". His mother tongue is "logudorese."

TOMMI AVICOLLI MECCA is a queer, southern Italian/American poet whose work has appeared in newspapers, anthologies and journals since the late sixties.

KAREN MELANDER-MAGOON is published in many anthologies, has sung major opera roles in Europe for two decades, and has five CDs online and video of her *Lillie, A Musical*. She is an interfaith minister and a co-editor of this anthology.

SARAH MENEFEE is an activist for the poor and homeless. She was a founding member of the League of Revolutionaries for a New America, the Revolutionary Poets Brigade, Occupy SF and First They Came For The Homeless.

TUREEDA MIKELL is a story medicine woman, poet and Black Panther alum, committed to voices of the people, published over 70 at-risk student anthologies, featured nationally and internationally. Her book is *Synchronicity: Oracle of Sun Medicine,* by Nomadic Press 2020,

GAIL MITCHELL, poet living in San Francisco, was featured in the full length film, *Passion is the Money*, and read not long ago at City Lights.

EDWARD MYCUE, born in Niagara Falls NY, and lived and studied in TX, MA, UC Berkeley, Elsinore DK, and Legon GHANA. His first volume of poetry was *Damage Within The Community* (1973), more recently *Mindwalking,* and his first online book is *I Am A Fact Not A Fiction.*

MAJID NACIFY, considered the Arthur Rimbaud of Persian poetry, was born in Iran in 1952, published In *the Tiger's Skin* in Persian, fled Iran in 1983 after the execution of his wife Ezzat in Teheran, and received a doctorate in Near Eastern Language and Culture at UCLA.

BARBARA PASCHKE, translator and poet, is a co-editor of this anthology. Her many multilanguage publications include *Volcan* (co-edited with Alejandro Murguia), *Clamor of Innocence,* and *First World Ha Ha Ha* (City Lights. She is a member of the SF Bach Choir and the Roque Dalton Cultural Brigade,

GREGORY POND, a prolific poet featured in many magazines and journals, currently hosts a poetry series at the CLARION Performing Arts Center in Chinatown, as well as organizing poetry sessions for the elderly. His work was recently featured in the Haight-Ashbury Literary Journal.

KATHY POWERS at the age of 50 realized her voice was the voice of the people, and became a revolutionary activist fighting to raise unheard voices. She lives in the Chicago area.

JERRY PRENDERGAST, a lifetime Chicagoan, has published his poetry often in *Blue Collar Review* and *Children Churches and Daddies.*

JAMI PROCTOR-XU is a bilingual poet and translator of Chinese. She is the recipient of a Zhujiang Poetry Award and a First Readers Poetry Award. Her translations of Song Lin's collection, *Sunday Sparrows* (Zephyr, 2020), received the Northern California Book Award for Poetry in Translation

NAZLEE RADBOY is the translator of Ziba Karbassi's poem in this anthology.

JÖRG W. RADEMACHER is a biographer, editor and translator, who composes occasional poems in three languages. He is the translator of the poem by Egon Günther in this anthology.

MARGARET RANDALL is an American writer, photographer, activist and academic. Born in New York City, she lived in New Mexico and for many years in Spain, Mexico, Cuba.

D.A. "ROARSHOCK" WILSON plays the harmonica, and picks a little banjo. He enjoys reading and publishing local poetry. Besides his day job, he dips and sells beeswax candles.

GABRIEL ROSENSTOCK Irish writer who works chiefly in the Irish language. A member of Aosdána, he is poet, playwright, haikuist, tankaist, essayist, and author/translator of over 180 books. He currently resides in Dublin.

SANDRO SARDELLA is an Italian poet and painter who has done major exhibitions of his painting, featured also in this anthology.

LUIS FILIPE SARMENTO Portuguese poet and filmmaker. Books: *40 Poemas 40 Pinturas: 40 Poems 40 Painting, The Intimacy of Sleep* (Water Mirror).

JOANNA SCANDIFFIO poet, educator and gemologist living in San Francisco. Her poems have been published in *Switched-on Gutenberg, Sugared Water.*

NINA SERRANO received the PEN award for *Heartstrong,* selected poems; Best Book Award from Artists Embassy. She produces *Open Book* on KPFA-FM radio, and *La Raza Chronicles*, and was one of the founders of the Mission Cultural Center in San Francisco.

KIM SHUCK is the 7th Poet Laureate of San Francisco Emerita. Shuck's latest books are *Noodle, Rant, Tangent,* a collection of essays, *Pick a Garnet to Sleep In,* a collection of poems, and This *Wandering State vol. 2,* an anthology in a series of anthologies from specific areas around California.

DINOS SIOTIS was born in Tinos, Greece, in 1944. He is editor of the literary magazines *(de)kata* and *Poetix*, runs the (de)kata publishing house, directs the Tinos International Literary Festival, and is currently president of the Greek Poets Circle.

DOREEN STOCK is a poet and activist, writer of *My Name is Y, a memoir of an anti-nuclear demonstrator*; she lives between Argentina and the SF Bay Area. Her other recent books are *A Noise In The Garden* (Kelsay Books, 2021), and *Your Excellency,*

Free Will (translations of Amparo Casasbella Alconada, with Marcelo Holot), Prosa Amerian Editores, Argentina, 2021.

MATTHEW TALEBI is a poet who lives in the Los Angeles area.

SARAH THILYKOU is a Greek poet, translator, essayist, book reviewer, and editor. Her publications include *Duet of Islands* (Kyoto 2018), and *Angelic Flights* (New York 2021).

RAYMOND NAT TURNER, is a NYC poet privileged to have read at the Harriet Tubman Centennial Symposium; he is artistic director of JazzPoetry Ensemble, UpSurge!NYC, which has appeared at numerous festivals and venues including the Monterey Jazz Festival and Panafest in Ghana, West Africa.

VIVIMARIE VANDERPOORTEN is Senior Lecturer at the Department of Language Studies, Open University of Sri Lanka. In addition to her own poem in this anthology, she is also the translator of the poem by Kusal Dhananjaya Kuruvitage.

DAVID VOLPENDESTA is a member of the Friends of Durruti, the Roque Dalton Cultural Brigade, and the San Francisco Revolutionary Poets Brigade. He is the author of *Forbidden Psalms* and is currently working on *Forbidden Psalms II.*

KARL WIENER is the artist of the graphic in this anthology connected to the poem by Gabriel Rosenstock.

CATHLEEN WILLIAMS is a Sacramento poet and editor of the newspaper Homeward. She is also a member of the San Francisco RPB.

D. A. "ROARSHOCK" WILSON is a San Francisco poet, author of *First Hours of a Rainy Day and Other Poems,* and publisher of *Roarshock Page,* a literary street flier. He reads regularly, locally and internationally, in person and via the social web, and can be found online at his website. www.roarshock.net

NELLIE WONG is a Socialist feminist activist and author of several collections of her poetry. Editor of *Talking Back Voices of Color* (Red Letter Press), she dreams in jazz, bards in Hoisan American dialect, and cooks for working-class solidarity.

ERIC ALLEN YANKEE is a member of the RPB/Chicago, an activist in the Chicago area, and is the author of the poetry collection, *Bees Against The War*.

LORENE ZAROU-ZOUZOUNIS is a Palestinian-American writer and poet. She writes poetry for all ages, prose, historical fiction for children & adults, short stories and science fiction.

ANDRENA ZAWINSKY is a Pittsburg born working-class poet and photographer who lives in Alameda, California; she is recipient of the Oakland PEN Josephine Miles Prize for her poetry.

REVOLUTIONARY POETS BRIGADE
MISSION STATEMENT

NOW
As poets we are uniquely positioned to seize the possibilities of the time, bringing language to life and participating in the movement that is gathering as we speak...

IT'S TIME
Poetry has always been and continues to be not only the way the poet listens to his or her innermost being, but a way the spirit of the times, in its most forward-looking incarnation, is expressed and heard. And the times we're in, of crisis and the cry for transformation, particularly needs the news, as poet W.C. Williams said, "without which we die."

We say what we see: and that is the system that cannot rest until it extracts every drop from a desperate earth: capitalism. We say what we see: and that is the oppression of our class, driven to the streets and alleys of our cities, driven to the muddy fields, all because there is no profit in maintaining life and health. We are the harbingers of revolution and the awareness that underlies and drives it.

FOR THE REVOLUTIONARY POETS
In our common struggle toward freedom, each individual instinctively reaches for the best tool at hand. As artists, we have the most powerful tool of all, the ability to inspire, transform, and liberate, just in the nick of time as it happens, as the sick old ways rust, choke, sputter, and fade. Poets, those at the compressed razor-sharp edge of

social thought, and all fellow artists of visionary courage, stay mindful of this historic opportunity, and lead with strong revolutionary voice for all humankind to genuinely live and thrive in common spirit!

BRIGADE
Therefore, we want to create a Revolutionary Poets Brigade, to respond to the demands of the moment – provoking the future out of the confused minds of today, inspiring with the passion of the living word, in preparation for the development on a wider and larger scale of the uprising, the action that will overthrow this system of greed and exploitation.

As a network, we can be present and participate in the popular resistance that is going on around us by holding poetry events, by reading and speaking at demonstrations, and by publishing broadsides and pamphlets. Join us.

"Camerados . . . will you come travel with us? Shall we stick by each other as long as we live?"
                                                    –Walt Whitman

REVOLUTIONARY POETS BRIGADE
http://revolutionarypoetsbrigade.org